A. KENDRA GREENE is an essayist, printer and maker of artist's books. She is a visiting artist at the Nasher Sculpture Center and a fellow at Harvard University's Library Innovation Lab.

THE MUSEUM

OF WHALES

YOU WILL

NEVER

SEE

Travels Among the
Collectors of Iceland

A. Kendra Greene

GRANTA

Granta Publications, 12 Addison Avenue, London W11 4QR

First published in Great Britain by Granta Books, 2020
This paperback edition published by Granta Books, 2021
Originally published in the United States in 2020 by Penguin Books,
an imprint of Penguin Random House LLC

The essays *Anatomy of a Museum*, *The Stone Collector*,
and *Vagrants and Uncommon Visitors* were originally published
individually as chapbooks, in different form, by Anomalous Press,
Boston & San Francisco, in 2015, 2016, and 2017 respectively.

A CIP catalogue record for this book
is available from the British Library.

1 3 5 7 9 10 8 6 4 2

ISBN 978 1 78378 594 0
eISBN 978 1 78378 595 7

Set in Arno Pro
Designed by Chris Welch
Offset by M Rules
Printed and bound by CPI Group (UK) Ltd, Croydon, CR0 4YY
www.granta.com

MIX
Paper from
responsible sources
FSC® C020471

For the sorcerer who took me to see petrified trolls,

who sent me running from the museum to catch a car departing

even before I understood that I might hope to see whales

Tears fall in all the rivers: again some driver
pulls on his gloves and in a blinding snowstorm starts
upon a fatal journey, again some writer
runs howling to his art.

—W. H. AUDEN, "JOURNEY TO ICELAND"

When they boarded the boats, the Icelanders had the
heaviest trunks. Because they packed their trunks with
books. Not clothes, not shoes. Books. You don't feel
starving or in pain if you have a book.

—VALGEIR ÞORVALDSSON

Why have a museum if you don't have a story?

—VALDÍS EINARSDÓTTIR

Reykjavik

Contents

Points of Reference

MASS AND WEIGHT

4 kilograms = 8.8 pounds = 16 merkur = the approximate weight of a human baby

20 tons = 40,000 pounds = the approximate weight of a red comb sea monster

DISTANCE

500 kilometers = 310 miles = approximate stretch of southern coast without a bay

ell = length of an arm from elbow to the tip of the middle finger ≈ 18 inches

40 ells ≈ 20 yards ≈ 18 meters ≈ length of a narwhal according to the 1585 Ortelius map ≈ 3x modern records of adult narwhal lengths

CURRENCY

800 kronur (ISK) ≈ $6.50 (USD) ≈ 6 euros (EUR) ≈ 5.5 British pounds (GBP) ≈ approximate cost of museum admission

3 cows = the cost of the first Icelandic language Bible, in 1584

TEMPERATURE

81 degrees Fahrenheit = 27 degrees Celsius = approximate peak recorded temperature in Iceland

SEASONS

By the old Icelandic reckoning, there are two seasons: summer and winter.

Summer begins the first Thursday after April 18. Winter begins on a Saturday in October, twenty-six weeks after the start of summer. Where I've taken the liberty of "spring" and "fall," they correspond to the time of year otherwise so named in climates of the Northern Hemisphere.

A Brief Introduction to Séríslensk Stafsetning, or Specifically Icelandic Orthography

As a student of Icelandic, you will become sensitive to the particular sounds and rules of letters like *á, au, é, ei, í, ý, æ, ö, dj, f, g, hv, j, ll, p,* and *r*; sensitive to the *y* sound that *j* makes, as in Reykjavík; and attentive to the trill of the *r*. As a tourist to Icelandic you might muddle through acute accents, but at the very least, you'll want a passing familiarity with eth and thorn.

The letter thorn (Þ in upper case, þ in lower case) is a survivor. It was popular in many historical languages, Old English included, but Icelandic is the only living language that still uses it. In shape it may resemble a pedestrian *p*, but it sounds like the "th" in "Thor," god of thunder and strength. Look for it in the bird name þórshani, or the last name Þorsteinsson, or the first names Þórður and Þorvaldur, and you can't miss it in the full name Þorbjörn Þórðarson. It is the soft, voiceless, almost whispered *th* of "thick" and "thin" and "thistle."

The letter eth (Ð or ð) shares ancient history with that runic letter thorn, and will come in handy if you have a

brush with Faroese or Elfdalian. It looks like Ð in the upper case, which won't come up much since it never starts an Icelandic word, but the lower case ð shows up plenty. It's there in towns like Siglufjörður and Bjarnafjörður and Ólafs-fjörður. It's there in basically every Icelandic home, though it's been centuries since anyone bathed in the room called baðstofa. There are those who would rather transliterate it to the visually similar *d*, but it is there nonetheless, making a voiced, vibrating *th* sound like "this."

THE MUSEUM

OF WHALES

YOU WILL

NEVER

SEE

Arrival

Lilja collects me from the airport bus under a gray morning sky and, swinging my bag into her little silver car, asks if I got her message not to worry about the volcano. "Because you shouldn't, and it won't affect your trip, and these things happen all the time."

The whole trans-Atlantic approach from Boston to Reykjavík takes less than five hours, which is scarcely time enough to fall asleep or start a third in-flight movie or convince yourself of the proper pronunciation of every unfamiliar letter in the Icelandic alphabet—eth and thorn, especially—but it is apparently long enough to board an airplane and cross half an ocean without having any idea you are aimed straight at a sudden increase in seismic activity.

Not that it should be surprising. Just the forty-five minutes from the international airport to the bus terminal downtown is a misty drive through old lava fields and venting hot springs, a gradual accumulation of houses and buildings tracing the ocean's edge of an island straddling two tectonic plates—an island that rose up from these waters in the first place precisely because of those plates, their penchant to slip and grind and spill their molten heart.

Lilja says, "Don't worry about the volcano," and in the same breath begins to describe the possibility of ash clouds and gas masks and helicopters plucking hikers from the mountains because there's no better way to alert them that they may be in mortal peril.

She pulls up the national weather service's website, teaches me to toggle from the outline of Iceland annotated with the forecast of rain, to the one predicting the visibility of the northern lights, to the dots and stars mapping a string of tiny earthquakes, every shift and shock detected for the last seventy-two hours. Mostly, on the map, they register not much more than a 3.0 on the Richter scale. I grew up along another shoreline, in California, and the freckling map prompts a certain kind of nostalgia, a tenderness for these almost imperceptible events.

I am to keep vigil, Lilja says. I am to refresh and refresh and refresh the map. It doesn't matter that they are tiny, doesn't matter that they are all but obscure. I am to watch whether the number of tremors waxes or wanes. I am to notice how their alignment is not random, every one of them a sign. I am to witness: Their accumulation, in fact, articulates the frontiers of fault line and fissure we cannot otherwise see. It describes those underpinnings shaping everything else. And, though we may tremble, it points us ever toward what may just happen next.

The ridgelines here are black rock or lupine laced, perhaps dotted with sheep, if not dusted with snow. Where there is shoreline enough I pick up sea glass and shards of china, walk past feathers and sometimes bones. I have come, I think it is right to say, because of the borders of this place. Because not just here but always, something happens at the edges.

I have come for the perimeter of territory staked out under the name "museum." Because for all the museums I have worked for or volunteered at or interned with, for all the continents where I have been the museum visitor, I have never known a place where the boundaries between private collection and public museum are so profoundly permeable, so permissive, so easily transgressed and so transparent as if almost not to exist.

"So maybe don't make plans until we know if the lava is melting the glacial ice, if the flood of all that water unbound will close the northern roads or the southern roads or, who knows—it's happened—both."

They say that if you're baptized wrong, if the holy water does not wash over your eye, you may retain another sight, may see the elves even when they do not choose to reveal themselves to you. And I feel something of that old story here, that I have been given a glimpse of something extraordinary, hidden though it was there the whole time, interwoven amid everything else we see or know or put in our pockets or hold in our hands.

Sometime later, in the calm of a museum café, I will be chatting with a family visiting from my homeland, and I will tell them how the local museum-studies professor puts the count at 265 museums and public collections in this country of 330,000 people, how that alone would be astonishing—but remember almost all these places have been established in the last twenty years, like seeds dormant forever and then triggered at last by some great fire, some sharp snap of frost, to finally take root and bloom.

Amazing, they agree, though they sit there in the museum café, sipping their coffees, never leaving the antechamber for the exhibits within. Outside, the mist collects and recedes, gathers up and blows through, the world beyond the museum's glass wall always there but veiled, disintegrating, fading in and out of perception's reach.

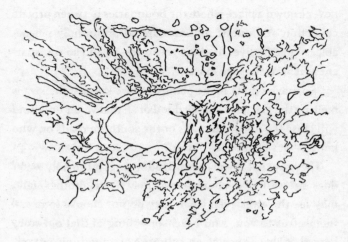

"And anyway it doesn't have to flood; it could spew ash. Maybe the crops die, maybe the sheep are poisoned, maybe you breathe through a washcloth and famine sparks the French Revolution."

These are old forces. The magma and the tremors. The famine and the want. The way we love rocks and birds and old boats and brass rings, and the way we survive this world because of the stories we fashion from its shards. We do not just keep and collect things, amass and restore them. We trouble ourselves to repurpose, create, and invent things just to carry, a little easier, those stories we cannot live without. Enchantments and mysteries and monsters and—the woman on the cusp of transformation searching for her sealskin so she can return home, become again what she was before—this is what we have always held on to, this is how we lash ourselves to the mast. These are old forces—irresistible, shaping the world anew.

The Museum of Something Mumbled

There was famine. And the family determined they could save one son by sending him away. Or maybe they determined that with one less mouth to feed, they could save themselves. So they arranged for his passage to North America, a very long time on a ship. As the sailing date drew near, the boy was too sick to journey—but everything was arranged and someone had to go, so they sent a different, even younger son in his place.

Relatives in North America dutifully met the ship, but when they could not find the name of the first son on the manifest, could not find the boy they had come for—and did not know to look for another—they went home emptyhanded. It did not matter when they learned of the substitution, if they learned of the substitution. No one heard from the boy who had been sent on the ship. No one was found who claimed they had seen him. No one could determine where the lost boy had died.

Only he wasn't dead. More than a decade after that first ship had docked, he stepped off another, returning home to Iceland, intent to find a bride. In all that time he'd never written. In all that time he'd never sent word. He had scarcely more to say in the flesh: something curt and mumbled about the native people, that they should be treated better, but no further accounting of his survival, of how that starving child became a man, standing here in a buffalo coat.

I myself know nothing more of him, of his story, would not know even this except for the buffalo coat, sequestered here in a glass case as if it had stepped into a phone booth to make a call. And even this, what little I know, feels misplaced, though it turns like a key in a lock.

It feels like a story not meant for me, in part because it hardly feels on display. It's not in the main museum but in an entry building, in a kind of hallway before temporary exhibits, at the far edge of the museum café. The coat has been given a footprint of text in its case, everything properly printed and kerned. It is a text shorter even than the story I tell here, the words in Icelandic but not echoed in another tongue, not a one of the other languages of the people who knew this man, knew the lost boy long enough for his shoulders to fill out this coat. I assume the text, too, says something curt and mumbled.

This is the story I was given, though I came looking for a reverend, after I was shown *that* man's frock and shoes. This is the story I was given after I kept asking about a different boat: the old fishing boat docked in sod and rotting on the museum lawn, never quite enough money to maintain it, now too dangerous to climb aboard, though anyone who grew up here used to clamber about its planks and railings as a child.

I keep this stray gem as one does any precious thing. I have the sense to hold close this story I did not come for, could not have asked for. I see the windfall immediately. This is the story I was given only after I was given the grand tour, after I was invited to rest in the museum café, after I thought my questions were answered, after I was given coffee and given cake, until I could eat no more.

ANATOMY OF A

MUSEUM

Icelandic Phallological Museum

(Hið Íslenzka Reðasafn)

t's different now. Whaling is legal again only recently—an industry shrunk until one family owns what whaling ships are left—but even though you can get it, people aren't used to eating the meat. It used to be a bounty. The whalers used to give away chunks of leviathan if you showed up at the whaling station and brought a bag to put it in. Plastic grocery bags, mostly. But if you had some garbage bags, if you had some friends, if you called ahead and the whale they had was the right kind of whale, if you brought your own ax, they might save for you a bit of flesh they couldn't use. And so you and your daughter might wrestle the penis of the whale—the tip, really, that third of it that extends from the body when, in death, the retractor muscles relax and the organ comes to equilibrium—wrestle its slippery dead weight into the backseat of your car.

THE FIRST ICELANDER I EVER KNEW WAS GARÐAR. GARÐAR was tall and blond and worked with my sister at a government lab in California. He volunteered to help hang the cabinets in her new kitchen, and as we sat on the concrete floor smoothing out installation diagrams, I confessed that I really didn't know anything about Iceland. I asked Garðar what he thought I should know.

It occurs to me now that he could have told me about the island skimming the arctic circle or having a total human population of 330,000 or the highest literacy rate in the world or a government agency just for making foreign words into Icelandic ones (cell phones named from an archaic word for a young sheep, the buzz of it reminiscent of a bleat). He could have claimed the singer Björk or the band Sigur Rós and left it at that. He might well have mentioned his namesake, the Swedish Viking Garðar Svavarsson, and that for some time Iceland itself was named after *that* Garðar. But he didn't say a thing about the years when Iceland was Garðarshólmi. He didn't bring up any of that. Right off the bat, with no further introduction, the one thing he told me about Iceland was this: "We have a penis museum."

"Really?" I asked.

"The only one in the world."

I LOVE A QUALIFIED SUPERLATIVE. BEST OR FIRST OR OLDEST is all well and good, but the oldest *continually operating* ice cream parlor in the world, for instance, the largest matchbook collection *in Europe*, the *second-oldest* museum *west of the Mississippi*—how much more charming are these claims for their tempered braggadocio, their peculiar specificity? And yet, in their precision they manage a curious elusiveness, keeping their calculations to themselves. Are we to suppose this is a humility born of the limits of even the most scrupulous research, that because there's just no telling what all exists in the world, honor dictates we claim no more than we can prove? Or do they know well and good the supreme matchbook collection of the globe is in Uruguay and they just aren't telling?

At their finest, these titles sound like niches narrowed and narrowed until there is no possible competition. Victory by exclusion! Glory by attrition! And still they are stated with such triumph, as though it were a most coveted distinction to be the regional self-proclaimed nearly almost sometimes runner-up.

By its own estimation, "The Icelandic Phallological Museum is probably the only museum in the world to contain a collection of phallic specimens belonging to all the various types of mammal found in a single country."

If any other institution is competing for this honor, it'll be hard to beat a small island country situated at the kind of extreme latitude that discourages biodiversity. Indeed, if the collecting mission were limited to just the *native* land mammals of a country, Iceland could have retired after the collection of one single arctic fox.

And why be limited to just mammals, one wonders. It's not biology. Fish are certainly fair phallus game, as evidenced by the Icelandic Phallological Museum's own display of two specimens of ocean perch. There are dragonflies with phalluses. And, sure, only 3 percent of bird species have any kind of phallus, but it's hard to dismiss them as negligible when the duck's penis is a corkscrewing tentacle of an organ that unfurls to a length equal to that of the duck's whole body.

But let's, for the moment, stick to the stated objective of mammals. It sounds straightforward enough, the Phallological Museum's collection a kind of mammal-phallus Noah's Ark—all the animals led in one by one—but in fact there's no official count for the number of mammal species in Iceland. On land you have to decide which of the introduced species count and whether your collecting mission expands with every imported exotic pet. In the water, you have to decide where Iceland ends and the open ocean begins. And then, even once you draw your borders, the ocean changes.

Forty or fifty years ago you wouldn't see a blue whale any farther north than the southern city of Reykjavík. Ditto for the humpback. Since then, changing water temperatures have drawn them farther and farther north, making them ever more present, while the right whale and the walrus are sighted less and less often. For that matter, there's less and less ice to float polar bears close enough to swim the rest of the way from Greenland. Historically they arrived often enough that there's official legislation about how to deal with them. As it is, the museum has one polar bear penis specimen: boneless, acquired late, that flesh the Icelandic Museum of Natural History didn't need when preparing their skeleton mount. Indeed belugas used to be spotted off the Icelandic coast, but no longer. The museum has no specimen to represent them. And likely never will.

SIGURÐUR HJARTARSON WAS BORN IN 1941, BACK WHEN Icelanders were still born as citizens of Denmark. In the 1950s he spent summers doing ranch work up in the north country, where one of the tools he used was a pizzle. If at the time no one paid much mind to a wizened, dried bull's penis being used as a whip, come 1974 it was an object of curiosity. By that time Sigurður was headmaster at a secondary school on the southwest coast, where he received a pizzle as a gift from a pupil's parent. He doesn't say why.

Sigurður has a master's degree in Latin American history. A textbook he wrote is still in use in Iceland's tenth-grade classrooms, and the summer we met he was translating an 1806 manuscript on the conquest of Mexico. He is a great visitor of churches and museums; when in Spain he always visits the Goyas at the Prado and a tapestry museum/workshop near the railway station. In 1977 he helped found Friends of the Arctic Fox, a conservation group that remains active to this day, and has written some fifty articles on the subject. Which is all just to say: A pizzle is not necessarily the obvious thing to give this man.

But I like to believe if you *were* going to give a whip to a headmaster, the pizzle would be your choice. Both its use and its origin suggest a certain violence and a commensurate authority, and yet to take it out of the country is to take it out of use, to render the dried old skin all the more impotent. Which makes the gift a bit ridiculous, a bite of satire under the mask of tradition. And as such it is a good gift after all; if Sigurður has been endowed with anything, it is a sense of humor.

Whatever the intent of the gift, its effect was inspiration. Not for Sigurður—he left it on a shelf in his office. But some of the teachers worked summers at a whaling station nearby, and once they knew about the pizzle, they started hauling whale penises into Sigurður's office. Which is to say, the initial expansion of the collection started as a joke. Imagine the strange satisfaction of plopping a giant penis across your boss's desk. Yes, it was a very good joke. And then, it's hard to say when, it became something more.

HERMES, BEFORE HE WAS A GOD OF TRAVELERS, WAS A GOD OF transitions and boundaries. Which I wouldn't think about much, even with the oceans warming and all the migrations rerouted, except that I once read about Alcibiades—that he was put on trial in absentia and sentenced to death for the mutilation of the Athenian hermai. Hermai, I should mention, are not people. A herm is a square- or rectangular-based prism of stone the height of a man with the head of a god and, here's the thing, male genitalia protruding from that prism in exactly the place you should find it if the prism were a body and not a slab. I have a certain affection for the hermai. I like to think, though it certainly is not true, that they represent a kind of missing link in the evolution of sculpture. I like to think first there were slabs and then there were busts and then, having mastered the head, someone decided to add the next most essential element, and later you get legs and then arms and before you know it we have—both at the National Mall and in the history of representational sculpture—something like the Washington Monument on one end and the Lincoln Memorial on the other.

When I traveled in Greece I did not meet the hermai at crossroads, which used to be their place, but in museums, where it was easy in my youth to dismiss them as juvenile or caricature or the work of an artist too lazy to finish the job. The hermai vary, of course—not even all of them are meant to be the god Hermes—but I encountered so many with their lascivious grins and lavishly exaggerated genitalia that in my earnestness and prudishness I could not take them seriously.

And yet, the first time I ever seriously thought about penises was in a Greek museum. Specifically, it was the national museum in Athens, where one bright March day our classics professor, Jörgen Ernstson, was wearing an ascot printed with tiny elephants and palm trees, and casually pointing out that the male genitalia represented in the statues of classical Greece were disproportionate to the rest of the figure. Too small, in fact.

Jörgen Ernstson had been trying to talk about identification, about how no one could tell if the bronze in front of us was Zeus or Poseidon because whatever the bearded fellow had been holding in his right hand was lost, and without that lightning bolt/trident/something else entirely, all we could really say was that the arms were too long for the body. We might have had a different conversation altogether if someone had brought up the eyeless eye sockets, but the group of young men in our cohort elected a representative among them and asked, instead, about the penis.

We can only guess that the arms are elongated because of perspective, to counteract an illusion of foreshortening, that the statue was not situated to emphasize wingspan but with the viewer in the same plane, directly in the path of whatever was being held up as if to be thrown. We don't know why the arms are so long, but there was definitely an answer for penis scale. At least for purposes of representation, the penis was considered by the Greeks if not exactly vulgar, then certainly something base. A constant reminder of the physical, the carnal, the hard to control. It was an animal attribute. Man in his ideal was a thing of reason, able to subvert the animal, and so there you had it: great men without great endowments.

The males in our group snickered. They'd been wondering for a while, actually, and were relieved to have an explanation. But it hit me differently. I hadn't noticed. Normally in a hall of nude statuary I'd find a way to casually avert my eyes, to draw attention neither to my looking nor to my not looking. But this new information made a difference. I felt the permission to look. Nay, not just look, but *scrutinize*—and not just permission, but obligation. Just the difference in belly buttons on figures at Zeus's temple in Olympia is enough to conclude that the pediment sculptures at the temple's front were made by one workshop and the ones facing away from the back by another. One must always pay attention, it turns out. So much depends on an outie. And penis size, I was shocked to discover, meant something after all.

THE DRINKING HELPED. YOU CANNOT RECEIVE A WHALE penis, I think we will agree, and not have your friends find out. Not in a town of five thousand people. Not when these are friends you drink with. And it probably does not matter that your friends are academics and members of parliament—someone is going to make a joke. Indeed, the jokes will get harder and harder to resist. Your friends will insert them everywhere. It's natural. There's no helping it. They'll become a handful. And no matter how erudite or innocent you imagine yourself to be, you will discover that everything is funnier when you talk about a penis museum. Eventually you will—you must—surrender to its charms.

And so it was at the bar in Akranes. Before you knew it, Sigurður and his friends were joking their way through the finer points of organizing an imaginary establishment. They coined an Icelandic acronym for the Phallological Museum: RIS/HIS, a play on words that translates as "rise happy." The English word *phallological* is Sigurður's own coinage, but he credits a colleague in the Latin department for describing the hypothetical institution as a *phalloteca*. They were always generous with one another, their contributions rewarded in honorifics from the nonexistent institution, until every one of them was pronounced, at the very least, an upright member in good standing.

None of this was raised as a serious possibility, of course. But that it existed as any kind of possibility, no matter how dubious, changed things. The Icelandic Phallological Museum became, if only remotely, possible. It had been given the special power of something with a name. The collection may have started with a whip, but the museum, I believe it is safe to say, was born at the bar.

They weren't necessarily accurate prognosticators. No one at the bar said, "Wouldn't it be great if your daughter and daughter-in-law had a bit of space in their children's clothing shop for your museum and you could sit whittling penis souvenirs while grading papers?" But so it went. The women were having trouble making rent, so they offered Sigurður half the roughly 3,800-square-foot storefront in a tidy little alley off Reykjavík's main shopping street. Sigurður was already in his third decade of collecting, and he had representations for thirty-four of the island's thirty-six mammal species sitting at home. So why not? He moved sixty-two specimens into his half of the shop, and the Icelandic Phallological Museum opened to the public on August 23, 1997. It was Sigurður's fifty-sixth birthday.

THE FIRST ARTICLE ABOUT THE COLLECTION WAS PUBLISHED seventeen years before there was any museum to visit. The early thrust of the collection was whales, and by 1980 there were thirteen specimens to report on. A Reykjavík paper decided to cover the penises under a headline that translates as 30KG WHALE PENIS DELIVERED IN A PLASTIC BAG.

When I ask Sigurður how a collection becomes a museum, he shrugs. It's the same reaction I get from the retired professor at the Volcano Museum, out on the Snæfellsnes Peninsula, or really from any museum anywhere else in this country. These things, he says, who knows? The local newspaper finds out you have an interest and they publish something, people ask to see what you've got, they make appointments to come over, and the whole thing matures, transitions. With every inquiry, the private collection becomes a bit more public. And then, one day, strangers are giving you money.

In Sigurður's case, someone from a local women's group might call to arrange a field trip, or a friend hosting a few foreign visitors would ask to stop by. In Iceland, a bachelorette party is not a stag party or a hen party but a "goose party," and the goose parties, too, started calling.

Maybe it means nothing (I'm almost sure that's so), but I

will note that all the museum's opening-night speeches were made by women. The men—all the writers and parliamentarians, the left-leaning, beer-drinking men who had been gabbing and joshing and prodding the museum along for years—were silent. They stood on the sidelines and clapped. It was as if by that time there was nothing left to be said. Their words had already done their work, given them this place to stand in, and perhaps that was enough to reckon with to leave them speechless.

Only one of them, a musician, had anything to offer up: an original composition he played later that night, when everyone had settled in, the speeches were over, and perhaps the less serious talk had resumed.

THE ICELANDIC PHALLOLOGICAL MUSEUM IS SMALLER THAN you'd think. The domestic collection of 212 specimens fits in one room. The combined sixty-four items in the foreign and folkloric collections share an oversize alcove. And yet, still, it is a little overwhelming. The first thing I do at the Icelandic Phallological Museum, moments after I have crossed its threshold, is pause long enough to collect myself, and visit the loo.

Even for those 60 percent of visitors who won't be using a phallus to relieve themselves, the water closet seems a natural introduction to the subject at hand—and the very architecture of the museum suggests the option. The main door opens to a landing, a small foyer presenting two options to continue on. Stairs up and to the left arrive at the museum galleries; stairs down and to the right (it sounds almost Freudian) deliver you to locked storage and the WC.

This is not by design. The design suggested for the museum, according to a cartoon in the archives, was a long corridor of a gallery met at one end by a pair of circular structures housing a gift shop in one lobe and a café in the other—a structure not unlike the actual design of Iceland's international airport, the aerial views of which were much commented on after its unveiling. No, that the museum should be housed in the peculiar architecture of Héðinsbraut 3a has only to do with the local bank, which offered the location to the museum for pennies on the dollar, glad to have something occupying the hundred-year-old house, someone to look after it and stop up its drafts.

The little signs marking the men's and the ladies' aren't of a set. The men's is a shingle of wood painted with a naked boy peeing into a bowl. The craftsmanship is a little rough, but the action is unmistakable. The ladies' room, on the other hand, is more discreet, mysterious, marked by a porcelain oval displaying a Victorian lady covered up from floor-touching hem to ruffled neck to gloved hands. Unlike the naked boy, she suggests nothing of the room's utility, hints coyly that perhaps behind that door you might—who knows what?—go for a stroll in the country, or adjust your boots without shamelessly flashing someone an ankle.

If you ask Sigurður why no vaginas, why not a museum of genitalia generally? He will tell you, with the wink of a man married some fifty years, "Women, in all things, are more complicated than men." He's not being arch. Well, he is, but there is a practical concern. It's already a technical challenge to display the emphatically convex, and what a museum can show has a lot to do with what it can keep. This museum, as much as it is anything, is a study in preservation. And preservation, especially here, is a series of experiments.

The first two whale specimens, a fin whale and a sei

whale, were filled with silicon, then salt to eat away the fat. Sigurður concedes, "I shouldn't have done that." But one has to do something, of course. Time is ticking. The curator chose, and chose quickly, and to be fair that choice has lasted forty years, even if now the skin of the sei whale is cracked down the left side in a meandering squiggle, the skin pulled apart like the banks of a lazy river.

A different sei whale phallus represents a different choice, the specimen bent in half and folded over itself to fit inside a canning jar capable of holding the volume but not strictly the length of its contents. Indeed, choices abound: Where one minke whale penis was hollowed, salted, dried, and placed on a wooden plaque, another was left whole, complete with retractor muscles and pelvic bones, to rest in its own aquarium like an aberrant nautilus, the glass plate covering it pregnant with cloudy drops of condensation, the internal tissues feathering the way cut cloth frays.

Every preparation in some way compromises how the specimen would have been in life. Disintegrating tissue clouds the formalin in flakes and fluffy blooms. The skin of a sperm whale specimen pulls away from its wooden core, a thin mottling black dermis and the rest gone to suede. A sixty-pound blue whale penis that once barely fit in the backseat is now shaggy and shriveled to one-third its size. Meanwhile, the formalin in another blue whale specimen's container has been changed three times to clear the blood and oil, most recently three years ago, and since then a layer of oil as thick as my finger has leached from the organ and coagulated so that it floats like a plate of amber, forty centimeters beneath the actual glass top.

Formalin works because it kills. It's terribly toxic. Drop the bottle of formaldehyde you're handling and you have five, maybe six seconds to get out of the room, out of the building. You always use it diluted. Just a 3.5 percent formalin solution is enough to keep a specimen forever; it kills whatever bacteria and fungi might otherwise decay the tissue. Sigurður had to get a permit to handle the stuff back in the 1970s, though no regulators have checked on him since.

It takes two or three days for the formalin to stiffen a specimen. Hopefully you've positioned it well. Hopefully you got it warm so you could draw out the blood. After the formalin has done its work, the specimen can be switched to storage in alcohol. But alcohol, although vastly safer, is more expensive than formalin, so not everyone bothers.

Sigurður, of course, has other collections. He collects books, music, bugs, pre-Columbian and indigenous South American art. Growing up, his four children and their friends were always most interested in the bug collection, despite the growing number of phallus specimens accumulating in the den. For a year the family traveled widely in Mexico, to museums and libraries and anything that caught their fancies. And with just a little cotton dabbed in formaldehyde, they subdued and collected all the tarantulas they wanted and more insects than they could name.

Insects, you will know if you so much as dust in the corners, desiccate exquisitely. They virtually dry themselves. When it comes to the simple illusion of enduring form, let us praise the desolate exoskeleton! And then let us bow our heads, and pity those curators ever endeavoring to preserve a pound of flesh.

THE FIRST THING I SEE WHEN I ENTER THE MUSEUM IS A half-naked man. Not a photograph or painting or sculpture of such a figure, but an actual man, a redhead, standing there with his shirt off. He's a fit specimen, early twenties, and as I top the stairs I notice there's a second man in exactly the same state of undress.

"Medium," they're telling the curator. The curator, who seems to find nothing out of the ordinary in this transaction, says nothing and steps into a back room. When he returns a moment later, the two shirtless Scotsmen pay for two T-shirts, the one covering himself in the IPM seal and the other donning a block of text listing the museum's name in seven languages.

The curator is organizing their kronur into the slots of a wooden cashbox carved from good Icelandic birch to resemble a phallus the size of a lunchbox. I am doing nothing so useful, and so they appeal to me to be their photographer. The redhead shows me where to stand, making sure the killer whale and the sperm whale specimens flank them in the frame. I click the shutter as the two men drop their pants.

The redhead, it turns out, is a zoologist. His friend is a biologist, and they need this picture because they're on a swim team. There's a tradition, they tell me, when on holiday, of posing in the team swimming briefs in front of monuments and tourist attractions: "The pyramids at Giza, the pyramids in Mexico, the Parthenon . . ."

"One guy got arrested in front of the White House last year," he says, with some combination of envy and pride. "We were hoping we'd get chucked out of here, so we could say, 'We got chucked out of the penis museum,' but the guy," he says, nodding to the curator, "he's too nice!"

Sigurður Hjartarson is written up more often for his gruffness—not for his quick wit or his handsome suspenders or the skulls in his study at home. After 131 articles and one documentary film about his museum, perhaps he's just tired of the same questions. Twenty-seven countries on at least four continents have published articles about the Icelandic Phallological Museum. The ones in languages I can read characterize the place as *weird, kooky, odd-ball, infamous, unique,* and *sadistic.* Mostly it's a matter of headlines, and it probably shouldn't bother me, but flipping through the museum's archives—nine scrapbooks on a bookshelf where *Whales, Dolphins and Porpoises* touches covers with *Sexualia: From Prehistory to Cyberspace*—I begin to take umbrage, to bristle at how rarely anyone seems to notice what an appealing little museum it is. It's curious, yes, but also engagingly exotic, comfortingly familiar, with chairs to sit on and printed guidebooks, and it's wisely sized to the average attention span. Plus, let's be frank here, it's not all that odd a place.

From a certain perspective, it's downright traditional. Without the individual collector or the amateur naturalist, what museums would we have? Both are fundamental and ever-present pillars of museum history. And anyway, novelty *itself* is a museum tradition. You want to see a human molar rooted in a rooster's skull like a bony comb? You want a hermaphroditic giant moth with one wing the size and pattern of a male and the other that of a female? You want a gemstone in a color you didn't know existed? A mineral formed of its own composition into a perfect cube? A tree trained and trimmed into a chamber you could walk inside? A note penned by Elvis Presley to Richard Nixon on airline stationery? Vintage valentines with racist punch lines? The web a spider spun in space? Every spoon a sanitorium inmate swallowed because a trip to the surgery was better than how she was living? You want to be surprised? You get yourself to a museum.

THE MUSEUM IS LIT, IN PART, BY A STRING OF SCROTUM SKIN lamps. We are standing directly beneath them when Sigurður points up. He has been explaining that it took him a while to find the right round form to stretch the skin as it dried. He points at an early one, and as I look up into the globe of it, I see geometry. I am trying to remember how small you can make a soccer ball when he asks if I recognize the pattern. The skin is denser where indented, glows darker at those folds, and it dawns on me that the lamp skin, by shrinking to the object that stretched it, has imprinted in the pattern of a handball.

There are penis shrines and penis sculptures and penis festivals the world round. You want sex, there's the Chinese sexual culture museum sixty miles northwest of Shanghai, the Musée de l'Érotisme in Paris, a dozen others in Amsterdam and New York and Tokyo and who knows where else. But this is no more a museum about sex than it is about urination. It is a museum not of function at all, but of form, and often then not even the complete apparatus intact, just what can be cut, what can be kept.

Perhaps this begins to explain why there are so few museums of specialized anatomy. There's the Nose Academy at the Museum of Student Life in Sweden's Lund University. There's a surgeon's personal collection of bronze casts made from celebrity hands on display in a Dallas hospital. If you hang around the Phallological Museum long enough, someone is bound to mention the woman in Europe planning a vagina museum, but it's to be a museum of vagina *art*, not vagina specimens. Or someone will inquire of the curator, "Do you know you have a colleague in the Netherlands?" A collector of testicles, it turns out. Animals only—the whole thing minor in comparison, and not even a museum.

Just as I am beginning to wonder when, exactly, comparative anatomy disappeared from the popular imagination—how we came to forget this science as old as the classical age, its contributions to evolutionary biology and phylogeny and comparative genomics, the life's work of Cuvier and Huxley, the foundation for Darwin, how Edward Tyson determined a porpoise was a mammal, and whales, too, and how that cracked open the world—the conversation has already moved on to geography. Did I know that the city of Tampere, in Finland, has a tradition of penis-shaped chocolates?

"They give them to the ladies."

This information is imparted to me by a resident of said Finnish city, a man who has just been taking pictures of his two sons. Photography is permitted in the museum. Visitors may flash all they like. The Finn has posed them, first the taller boy, then the shorter one, next to Specimen A2h: an adult sperm whale beached alive in Hrútafjörður in the year 2000. The whale was 15.8 meters long at death, and died from an intestinal blockage. Only the tip of the penis was taken, yet at 170 centimeters and 70 kilograms, it's both a popular inducement for portraiture and a little bigger than most of the people who have their picture taken with it. If it were brass, there would certainly be a bright shine on its tip and a band around the back where visitor after visitor would drape an arm around it like some old school chum and grin. Visitors are as well behaved here as in any museum, but I notice that the women, especially the women, touch things. The men, I observe, prefer to take pictures.

The Finn leaves a card at the curator's desk, says to give the chocolatier a call, maybe they'll donate a mold. He gathers up his boys and his camera gear and heads toward the door. In parting he mentions, as if anyone was wondering, "They make them in white chocolate, too."

WHERE THERE ARE JARS, THEY ARE CAPPED WITH EVERY kind of lid: jars of jam and mustard and pickles washed out and filled with specimens, the metal lids twisted back on and taped shut. There are canning jars, sealed with their orange rubber rings. If it weren't for the labels, I'd believe a collection of sea slugs and tubers had been mixed in with the penises, so many of the shapes more familiar to me as aquatic fauna and flora.

Capra hircus, the goat specimens, are notably hairy. They look like animals unto themselves, like little opossums curled up and sleeping. The dried phallus of an old boar mounted on a rock looks exactly like some springing desert wildflower. The skunk's penis bone has the lilt and lobe of a day lily's anther, while the penis bones of young Greenlandic seals are as thin and tan as matchsticks.

Perhaps because it's housed in a glass jar and metal lid identical to the set storing the rotten phallus of a long-finned pilot whale, five jars over, I assume a narwhal tusk is just another baculum until I read its label more carefully and realize the ivory taper is not a penis bone but a tooth. Sure, it's a tooth most likely from a male—though sometimes the females grow them, too—but why is it here?

Add to this mystery my occasional disappointment. Who would ever know from the four feline penis bones on view that the fleshy phallus surrounding the bone is barbed? As long as we're talking about penises, isn't that a thing worth knowing?

THE IMPORTANT THING IS TO LISTEN TO THE NEWS. THE news will report whale strandings and polar bear landings, and then you make a few calls. But it works in reverse, too: People call the museum and then the museum makes the news. "We have a walrus," the caller says, or the boat's just brought in something. A farmer up the road loses his prize stud and asks to make a donation in memoriam.

Nobody talks about it as a collaboration, but the collection is and always has been contingent on its contacts, a series of dots connected. Sigurður would have a better polar bear specimen except, as he says, "Greenlanders are worse than Icelanders—they *never* answer a letter."

In the end, most things come by accident of fate. Once, some Icelanders were consulting to the sugar industry in South Africa, where an elephant with a sweet tooth had become a nuisance. If an elephant takes a liking to the cane, there's nothing to stop it from forever trampling the green-magenta fields and eating its fill. If you are the elephant, this is nirvana. If you own the field, you kill the elephant. After this particular elephant was killed, some local guys cut off the penis of the dead pachyderm and were playing with it, knocking it around like a soccer ball, when the Icelanders intervened. We can do better, they said. We have an idea. The ad hoc footballers gave up their prize, and the Icelanders made some calls. The curator put up six thousand kronur for the taxidermist to do the prep work and paid six times that to ship the African offering up to the North Atlantic. Iceland has strict laws about the importation of meat, but bones and preserved specimens come through customs just fine.

In some ways, the specimens themselves are not half as remarkable as the fact that they can be collected in the first place. Imagine: You can drop by a whaling station or call up someone you read about in the paper, arrive with a sharp blade and a container, and go home with a specimen. Strangers call from around the world. This guy, he loved this ram—it had given him more than two hundred sheep—and when it died he phoned the curator to ask, "Do you want his specimen?"

No animal has ever been killed for the museum. But if you know a hunter or a trapper or the crew sent to dispatch a rogue polar bear, what's the harm in asking for what they won't use? Who's to miss such a small bit of mink?

WHEN SIGURÐUR RETIRED FROM TEACHING IN 2004, HE moved to the northern coastal town of Húsavík, and he took the museum with him. In postcards of the original museum space in Reykjavík, there are little pictures of whales near their labels. In the museum's Húsavík incarnation, even that bit of context is stripped away. I can't tell you what an American marten is, but I have seen its penis. I know this because each specimen is marked with a little green sticker dot, like tags in a yard sale.

The dots adhere to various jars and mounts and frames, and their code of letters and numbers translates reliably to listings in the guide available at the front desk. The museum guide is printed in six languages, each bound separately in color-coded covers. To guess by the curl of their pages, the preference is for: German, English, French, Icelandic, Italian, and Spanish, in that order. Visitors ask with reasonable frequency for Russian, Croatian, Finnish, and Lithuanian, but as of yet the languages of the Icelandic Phallological Museum remain those languages that were taught at the school where Sigurður was when he opened the museum, every department chipping in their share. Sigurður claims there are in fact three languages of the IPM: "Icelandic, which hardly anyone speaks; Latin, which nobody speaks; and Esperanto, which nobody speaks—but everyone should."

The founding specimen of the collection, the pizzle, is marked "D-10-a," which corresponds to the additional information in the guide: "young adult bull, tanned, was collected in 1974." The specimen hangs on the wall between a testicle lampshade and a passage from part one, act six, scene four of Shakespeare's *Henry IV*. There are passages from Melville and the *Oxford English Dictionary* posted on other walls, and folkloric specimen PF119, the elfin ram, cites a novel by Iceland's Nobel Prize winner in literature, Halldór Laxness. But besides the bard and the laureate and *Moby-Dick*, in general, the walls are mute. If you want to know anything more than what you can see, you have to carry the words with you.

THE SECOND-LARGEST TOWN IN ICELAND HAS THIRTY thousand people in it, and the rest have a small fraction of that. Yet there is no shortage of museums throughout this country. Stranger still, when I start asking, it's hard to find a museum in Iceland that opened before the 1990s. It may signify nothing more than a long-poor nation finally growing wealthy. It may have to do with islands and isolation and identity. Certainly no one connected to the museums, not one soul, will countenance any motivation having to

do with tourism or com-
merce. But at least anec-
dotally, it seems like
something must have
happened in the recent
past to cause Iceland its
bloom of museums.

In his paper "Glo-
balized Members: The
Icelandic Phallological
Museum and Neolib-
eralism," anthropolo-
gist Sigurjón Baldur
Hafsteinsson links the
creation of the Phallological
Museum to what he identifies
as the ideologies of the government elected in 1991. Party policies
stressed entrepreneurship, commercialization of the culture
industry, and enhancing the entertainment value of cultural
practices. They also supported individual freedoms, including sexual freedom. At the Phallological Museum, Sigurður
cannot identify any shifts in culture that influenced his decision to start the museum, any particular policy or impetus,
but he does say this: "I wouldn't have tried it twenty years
before."

There are three museums in Húsavík, all of them rather
recent. The Húsavík Whale Museum opened in 1997, followed in 2002 by the combination natural history/folk/
maritime/art museum and district archives known collectively as the Húsavík Culture House, and in 2004 by the
Icelandic Phallological Museum.

At the Culture House I learn about tin water wings and how your breath can freeze in your beard until you have to saw off your mustache in order to breathe. I learn: "Thus, in Icelandic, a piece of unexpected good luck is often called 'hvalreki'—'a whale stranding.'"

I am thinking about *hvalreki* in the Húsavík Whale Museum, which bills itself as the "only museum in Europe dedicated exclusively to whales and whale related topics" and is a place that had the testicles and penis of a harbor porpoise on display even before the Phallological Museum came to town. I am thinking about when an adult whale beached itself on the northwest coast in November 1997, having already survived for quite some time without benefit of a mandible, and how it would become a boon to two Húsavík institutions. The jawless skeleton went to the Whale Museum, and the penis, plus one testicle, to the Phallological Museum, now just up the street.

THE WHOLE OF ICELAND USES ONE PHONE BOOK. THE national population of 330,000 fits comfortably in one volume and, as if to suggest that everyone knows everyone anyway, the listings are done by first name. I'm told this has less to do with the tremendous familiarity among inhabitants of a small island than with the simple practicalities of a patronymic naming system. In Icelandic tradition you take your last name from your father, so parents only rarely have the last names of their children, and siblings have different last names according to their gender, such that my brother would be a Warrensson, and I'd be a Warrensdóttir.

It takes days at the museum for it to dawn on me that this convention allows for a certain kind of deduction: that the artist Þorgerður Sigurðardóttir must be some Sigurður's daughter, and most likely the Sigurður in question is the curator himself. I had been thinking about the artist Þorgerður Sigurðardóttir because of her sculpture *Our Silver Boys*, installed on the museum's north wall. It is elegant in its austerity: fifteen silver casts representing the Icelandic national handball team, stood upright like striving mushrooms and collected in a vitrine twice the size of a shoe box.

You have to understand that the handball team is famous here, famous like a boy band, with Icelanders able to name each and every member. When they took silver at the 2008 Olympic Games, it was a very big deal for this one–phone book nation. And it gave Sigurður an idea. One of the Olympians was a former student of his and the son of a colleague. One phone call to the player's mom and Sigurður had the phone number to call the team in Beijing. It was loud in Beijing. The player answered, but it was hard to hear over a room in jubilation. And though everyone seemed agreeable in these initial talks, the actual logistics of organizing fifteen superstars to sit (stand?) for a mold to be made of each of their penises proved difficult.

I should say it is a lovely installation. Pithy, even. How simply does it point up issues of masculinity, and competition, and the intersection of personal and national pride? It's a witty observation on penis as trophy, not to mention a subtler reference to issues of gender identity and sex segregation in athletic arenas. It's more than just a novel commemoration of a small country medaling on the world stage—but even at that, it's really pretty great.

One day, after I've been hanging around long enough, Sigurður suggests I pull up a seat. He clears away some stacks of info sheets to make a spot on the desk for us to enjoy afternoon cookies and apple juice. Over three days we work through a box of Haust Grahamskex, breaking each waffle-patterned whole-wheat biscuit in half, eating them slowly. When I ask him about *Our Silver Boys*, he throws me a few one-liners. "No, they aren't in the same order as the picture," he says. And, "I won't say which one is which, but I think their wives could tell you!"

Then he tells me something that sounds at least as true. When he couldn't get all the medalists together to make the molds, Sigurður asked his daughter to make fifteen ceramic models of various lengths and lilts. And then, after much searching, they discovered a silver-colored car paint. It approximated the element convincingly, made the ceramic shine like metal.

WITH A LITTLE MORE GENEALOGY I LATER SURMISE THAT Embla Magnúsdóttir is not just the twelve-year-old artist behind "Facies Clarae Emblensis (Famous Faces)"—a collage rendering of Justin Timberlake's head atop a long, limbless body cut from a magazine's slick pink page—she is also Sigurður's grandchild, the daughter of his son-in-law Magnús.

In addition to its catalog of specimens, the Icelandic Phallological Museum has a separate guide covering "Works of Art and Other Artistic Oddments," which are on display throughout the museum. The guide lists 207 items, with their faux Latinate names in parentheses. Take number 12, for example, *The Desirable Marzipan Man* (*Homo gastronomicus Marsipanicus*). And number 13, *The Christmas Soap* (*Homo jabonicus natalicus*). It's an exotic roll call altogether: *The Philippine Ashtray, Barcelona Spoon; The Canary Islands Nipple, The Camden Clothes Hanger; The Danish Bottleopener, The Urinating Portuguese.* The distant nation of Papua

New Guinea has yielded not one but two phallic sheaths: one for festive occasions, and one for everyday use. Modesty forbids further explanation of *The Golden Birthday Present* or the *Very Masculine Apron*, but let it be said, they are not among the packages the curator has received and rejected as too vulgar, as so thoroughly lacking in artistic value that they had to be thrown away.

As I read the museum's Oddments catalog, Sigurður's family connections come into sharper focus. One daughter brought home the *Thailand Medieval Jewel* and *The Self-conscious Chinaman*. Another daughter and two grandchildren returned home with *The Columbian Love Play* and *Two Cocktail Straws*. For Christmas one year, the curator unwrapped the *Gentleman's Willy Care Kit* and *Columbian Indian Penis Flute*, from a granddaughter and a grandson, respectively. *The Pink McDonalds Man* (*Homo rubicundus McDonaldensis*) is a gift from the curator's grandson after visiting a McDonald's in Reykjavík. There is no longer a McDonald's anywhere in Iceland, a thing that left more or less when the US military decamped, yet this artifact is preserved. *The Flyman* (*H. operimenti Karsnesius*), a triangular seated figure, was carved by the curator's youngest daughter, Lilja, when she was thirteen, and it has been part of the collection ever since.

I meet the grown Lilja, a woman the age of my older sister, when she comes to watch the museum for a week. The museum is open 114 days a year, from late May straight through early September, which is much too long for one person to work continuously, so the curator's children each take a turn to relieve him. The rest of the year, when the museum is closed but Sigurður is still in town, entrance may still prove attainable. The curator leaves a note on the door with his cell phone number. Appointments, the note says, are available for the "very eager."

"They always call," Sigurður says, though of course there's no way for anyone to know.

Lilja is a novelist with short blond hair and her father's great blue eyes. The day we meet she is wearing wool earrings made by her sister, and they bob as she nods that, yes, the collection has inspired gift giving from the family for decades. I think of my own father, a pharmacist turned lawyer who always has a book about language or politics or regional history on his nightstand. Through no fault of his own, he has always been the most challenging person in the family to buy gifts for. My brother and I, in a moment of genius, once realized that we didn't have to pick his gifts on mere tradition or our mild hunches. So we asked him what he liked, and he said, after some reflection, "Deposing doctors." We fantasized about putting a doctor with a big red bow under the tree for interrogation. Instead we bought him another book. Which is to say, if Sigurður weren't a curator, if he didn't have this collection to run, who would know what to give him for his birthday? Honestly, it would be a problem.

IF YOU ASK SIGURÐUR, HIS FAVORITE PART OF THE MUSEUM IS the Folkloric Collection. It's certainly among the oldest; its roots go back to the pub. In terms of size, it's the most modest of the Phallological collections: a single case of twenty-one specimens that fits in a corner in an alcove otherwise dominated by foreign phalluses, right beside the American black bear and the tammar wallaby and the pygmy shrew.

Although it's a small collection, it's a pretty comprehensive alternative primer of Icelandic mythology. Within its glass case you'll find the phallic specimen of the one-eyed, one-armed, one-legged beach murmurer. There's a jaunty Icelandic yule lad "found deceased at the foot of Mt. Esja near Reykjavík on January 6th 1985. Presented to RIS-HIR by a former mayor of Reykjavík on January 6th 2000." The misfortunes of Epiphany aside, there are also sea howlers and shadow hounds and a beach walker, "found in SE Iceland in 1848 by Jón Magnússon, who was said to be 'truthful, re-spectable, restrained, and acceptably intelligent.'"

Indeed, there's a merman, a sea bull, a water horse. Good-ness, there's a whirler, a changeling, a foxacat. Imagine: the nasty ghost of Snæfell and the corpse-eating cat of Thing-mull! The enriching sea mouse, come to that! And all of it, if you didn't know better, is represented in stones and bones and gourds and wood. The specimen of a huldumaður, or hidden man, is suggested only by a jar filled with fluid and nothing else. It's the gift of a member of parliament. Sig-urður promises me it's there.

A FRIEND TELLS ME THAT WHEN SHE WAS A LITTLE GIRL AND all her friends were boys, she once dreamed that their pe-nises started to rise and swell, grew bigger and bigger, en-veloped their legs until they were mermen and, flipping their penis-tails, they swam away in the dirty ditch water. What she remembers is how lonely it was when they left. If this is not folklore, if this is not myth, then I want some new collection, some cabinet for tails and dreams and awe and dread.

LILJA SAYS SOME FEMINISTS LIKE THE MUSEUM BECAUSE IT takes the phallus off its pedestal, shows it as just another thing in the world, stripped of its mystique. Which is fascinating, given that the specimens quite literally *are on pedestals*—if they aren't mounted to the wall like trophies or set up in monumental prisms too big to be raised off the floor. And never mind the legendary and mythical ones.

But of course they're right, the feminists. What's interesting about the Icelandic Phallological Museum is this: It's a museum about a word. A word charged and freighted in ways that so very often have nothing to do with the biology of the thing it names. Touring the museum, every physical specimen is a reminder of the distance between the actual thing a word like *penis* describes and all the other things those words connote. It's sort of an embarrassing disconnect. How shabby of us, in the bluster of association and innuendo, to have constantly invoked the myth while stubbornly neglecting to consider the plain, bald fact of blood and flesh and skin.

More broadly, this is a museum of language, of expectations, of what one imagines a phallological museum to be, and the dry joke of what it turns out to be. The joke: It is exactly what it claims to be. Wall-to-wall penises. Maybe the odd testicle here and there, some art and some artifacts, but mostly it really is just a big old room full of penises.

You arrive prepared to be shocked, but it turns out what's startling is that someone has dared dedicate a museum to something so common—the penis presented not as vulgar, but as ordinary. Indeed, how easy to forget there are other penises in the world. If you don't happen to wear a raccoon's penis bone for luck or buy a souvenir oosik in Alaska, you've probably never conceived of a baculum. And even then, with one slipped into your pocket or the walrus's bone packed on the diagonal to fit in your checked luggage, you probably don't know the word *baculum*, much less the simple fact that most male mammals have these penis bones, including every primate but us.

It's a neat trick, the double inversion of expectations. You go to the museum, I think, because you hear "phallological museum" and you can't believe that what you imagine actually exists. And, sure enough, it doesn't. You know as soon as you walk in the door that you had it all wrong. It's not salacious. It's not even funny, except that the joke is on you.

But if the museum is not what you'd imagined could exist, it is something better. It is the gift of something you could not have imagined on your own.

Indeed, you wouldn't want it to be what you were imagining. You are glad to find it so sober. This is a museum of substance. Its gift shop is small and mild: forty postcards, T-shirts in two designs, a few books, and the scrotum-skin lamps. Until recently you could get birch key chains sculpted by the curator's own hands. Yes, whatever you were expecting, it is more surprising and fulfilling to discover something charmingly stranger yet. Lo and behold, comparative anatomy, that old science, really *is* kind of illuminating—you weren't expecting that.

LAST SUMMER IT HAD TO BE BAROQUE. NOW IT'S BEETHOVEN'S piano concertos and string quartets, two compact discs traded in and out of the machine all summer until they break. The CD player is tucked away next to the desk. Above it, there are two calendars on the wall—one of Greek red-figure pottery, the other of Che Guevara adjusting a camera—but nothing marked on them to distinguish one blank-square day from the next. Sigurður stands next to the empty calendars drawing tally marks in a notebook as each visitor arrives. "Eight hundred kronur," he says, then to complete the couplet, "Cash only." Because only in this museum and on the city bus does one ever need hard currency in Iceland. He makes one statement and then the next, repeated like a chant, a hundred times a day.

"Haven't you got anything smaller?" he asks visitor after visitor trying to tender a five-thousand-kronur note, and I wonder every time he asks if that's a penis joke, but no one ever laughs. It used to cost half as much, the price of admission rising slowly over time until the museum finally broke even in 2008. Since then, Sigurður figured, as long as he's not losing money, there's no reason to go higher. You can tell from the tally marks in the admission book that every year the museum gets busier, though the start and the close of the season are always slow. Still, it adds up. Over the course of the summer, Sigurður will mark down some thirteen thousand visitors, one tally at a time. It's a curious reward for so much originality and spontaneity and language play: to build a museum and then stand there entombed in the endless repetition of basic administration.

I have a friend who says the difference between a collection and a museum is interpretation. We were discussing this in another Icelandic museum, a place I love in no small part because its name is variously translated as "The Museum of Small Things" and "The Sundry Museum," and because it's the kind of place to display a few dozen thick and rustic antique nails arranged bristling from an ancient whitewashed board like a hedgehog in prototype.

The Museum of Small Things exhibits not just nails but also keys, so many keys, and telephones, and every pencil to come into the collector's possession since he started school. My friend is an architectural historian, and I have managed art collections, and we were both very fond of a text panel quoting the collector as saying of the things he might collect, "If it's not old now, it will be."

But my friend wasn't willing to grant the Small Things collection status as a museum, no matter what it wanted to call itself. Hoarding is not curating, she said. Sheer mass does not make a museum. Museums, she suggested, are collections sorted and arranged into stories, given order and explanation and sense. Collections, by themselves, are just groups of things.

It's a useful distinction, I think. And I wonder, as a practical matter, if we wouldn't have more museums but for the dearth of people who can entertain such wholly different capacities—who can both embrace the ecstasy of acquisition, and then sit around cataloging, taking tickets, sweeping up, explaining over and over again that it's too big a bill to break.

THE SUMMER I VISIT THE PHALLOLOGICAL MUSEUM, Sigurður is turning seventy. It's his last summer, indeed his last weeks, with the museum. "Will there be a big closing party?" I ask.

"No," the curator says.

When the Chilean periodical *Las Últimas Noticias* asked Sigurður in 2007 what he would do with the museum in the advent of his death, he said he didn't know. "Posiblemente lo donaré a la Iglesia Luterana de Islandia." *Possibly I'll donate it to the Lutheran Church of Iceland,* he said. The Lutheran Church has yet to express an interest, but Sigurður has had plenty of other offers over the years. In 2010, some Icelanders wanted to buy the museum and modernize it, do a redesign with some museum architects in Reykjavík. But it's not for sale, not to them. Too dicey. Too much risk it would change into something pornographic, leering, something it wasn't meant to be.

So instead, when Sigurður retires, his only son will inherit the museum, move it all back to Reykjavík, and make a go of it there. Mostly it will be the same: all the same specimens, all the same labels. The same hand-carved cashbox, the same chant of admission. But we can, at least, expect a more developed gift shop under the son. "He has a better head for business," Sigurður says.

Lilja says, "My father, he can't be bothered," nodding at the bookcase that passes for a gift shop. "Unlocking the case, giving people change . . ." He just doesn't attach much importance to it. Time was he had the interest to sculpt phallic door handles and coat trees and gavels. In the year 2000 you could buy a skipping rope with wooden phallus handles for just twenty-six dollars, but Sigurður stopped carving two or three years ago. The key chains he can outsource to Indonesia (now in three different colors of wood), but the salt and pepper shakers have become only a collector's item. If you want so much as a back scratcher, I'm sorry to say they're out.

I ask Lilja if there was any dissent in the family on the decision to give Hjörtur the museum, but she assures me that she and her sisters were of one mind. Yes, the sisters have all been donors to the museum, they all love the place—heck, the eldest had a lovely pagan wedding in its galleries back in 2003—but the women were in agreement: This was a museum that could be handed only from father to son.

THE COLLECTING WILL GO ON. OF COURSE IT WILL. POISED to retire in a month and a half, the curator still had a wish list: polar bear (better), blue whale (more complete), pure Icelandic dog. One can always upgrade the specimens for species already represented in the collection, and the scope of the collection can always expand to include new species. If only there were some Ahab to bring them in, some sea animals have phalluses that are meters long. A complete foreign collection could be the life's work of another man— or, ahem, men. The domestic mammal collection alone was completed only in April 2011.

In the most polite terms, Páll Arason was what Sigurður calls "a famous guy." A pioneer in Icelandic tourism, Arason was "the first or second person" to take tour groups to the Highlands, the island's beautiful and capricious interior. An old hippie once rapturously described to me glimpses of the highland rocks shaped like petrified trolls, and I hear it's an exceptional place to travel by horse, though the rain and the sleet will come at you without warning and there will be nothing to do but soldier on until it stops. In fact, when I pick up my rental car, there is a cardboard map of the country covering the steering wheel, illustrating in two colors where I may and may not take this tiny white vehicle with its manual transmission and its nominal backseat. A thin blue perimeter rings the island, the permitted paths ignoring the whole of the Highlands and its bad roads and bad weather and no towns to stop in anyway. The map does not specifically indicate that thar be dragons, or lake monsters, or witches or trolls, but still I leave the Highlands to the discretion of drivers with, if not more adventurous souls, then certainly more rugged means of transport.

Arason was admired as an adventurer, but he was also known as a political fascist and an infamous womanizer. The press sometimes prefer the word *Nazi*, as in the headline:

SE CORTÓ EL PENE DEL NAZI! *This curator cut off the penis of a Nazi!* Whatever else Páll Arason may have been, he was well documented as the first person to pledge the museum a human specimen. He was eighty years old at the time. Sigurður was then two species shy of collecting every mammal in Iceland. The collection wasn't even a museum yet, would open later that year, but Arason's intent to be a posthumous donor was signed and witnessed.

Arason had been old when he made the agreement, but he lived longer still, long enough to notice a decline in his nineties, long enough to note that, as a specimen, his penis was no longer the legacy he had intended to leave behind. He lived long enough to reconsider. In the meantime, the museum had nothing to show but the legal paperwork of a promised gift. Well, technically, the museum had a human foreskin on display, plus the testicles of a separate donor, but without a complete phallic specimen from *Homo sapiens*, the curator considered the collection wanting.

As time went by, three more men volunteered, younger men: an American, a German, and a Brit. Their deeds of gift, too, went up on the gallery wall. The curator did not think too hard about whether they represented a domestic species or a foreign one. And then at the start of 2011, fifteen years after signing, Arason passed away.

You might think that in those fifteen years, there was time to prepare, ample time, an excess of time, time abundant and time runneth over. The legal work, after all, was so tidily done. Everyone knew his wishes. The museum had prepared 275 specimens before this one. And yet, when Dr. Peters called late on the winter night of Arason's death, what he asked was: "What should I do?"

A sober Sigurður would have said, "Get it here fresh!" A sober Sigurður would have advised, "Use two to three teaspoons of vinegar to draw out the blood." It's the blood that leaks out and stains the preserving fluid, but if you siphon it off in the first place, there's nothing to do but preserve the specimen, posture it, dip it into its formalin bath. But in the middle of the night, there was some confusion. Mistakes, as they say, were made. Sigurður calls it the "tragedy of Mr. Arason. Terrible, terrible." He vows to make amends.

I myself hate to look at it. The museum's smallest specimen is less than two centimeters, a hamster's penis bone, and I will happily stare at that with the provided magnifying glass, noting as I do that the specimens of the house mouse and the black rat are all but imperceptibly bigger. But contemplating the human specimen in the same case is viscerally unpleasant, in a way that only unrecognizable things can be.

Fortunately, the human donation, specimen D-15-b, is easily missed. Toured clockwise, the main gallery ends at the grid of cubbies you pass coming in. There are the three human contributions together, underneath the mink specimen cubby and right between the dog cubby and red fox cubby. The human phallus is flanked by a jam jar of foreskin, specimen D-15-a, and a bell jar of testicles, specimen D-15-c. A young boy standing with the famous specimen no more than six inches from his chin turns to ask his mother, "Which one is it?" She checks the catalog and points to the appropriate vessel and the boy jerks away in shock.

"That's not really what it looks like," his mother agrees.

As they walk away, the young boy's younger sister adds matter-of-factly, "It's probably the *inside*." She is wearing pigtails, and she looks so confident in this consolation, so very assured that everything is right after all, that I dare not say what strikes me as the obvious thing: Nothing on the inside would be so hairy.

ANOTHER DAY, A DIFFERENT SMALL BOY SEES THE SCROTUM skin lamps and declares: "I want to eat one."

It's a day when Lilja's at the museum, and she leans over to me and whispers, "He's out of luck—wrong season." If it were January or February, she tells me, I could pop out and pick up pickled ram's testicles at any old supermarket, but here in July we'll just have to wait. Instead, a few weeks later in Reykjavík, we dine on brown bread ice cream from her mother's recipe, and pungent cubes of decomposing shark.

Her father, on my last day at the museum, had reminded me to try whale before heading home. An acquired taste, perhaps, the curator said, but an essential one. Were I an Icelander, it would be my generation that grew up without the taste of whale, without the ritual of eating it, the ones who are having trouble finding their way back. Even now, when I drive past the old whaling station near Akranes, it's hard to tell it's still in business, that the gray buildings and the chains on the fences are anything more than a dead industry clotted against the fjord. But perhaps it's always looked this way, perhaps it was just the same when Sigurður brought his daughter there years ago, the same striking, impish woman who orders the shark and now watches me lift a bit of rotted flesh to my lips with a toothpick (because you can't get the stench off of silverware), watches eagerly as the taste begins tolerable but then the tender pale meat blooms foul with ammonia and I must throw it back or spit it out.

You would think the old traditions are strange because

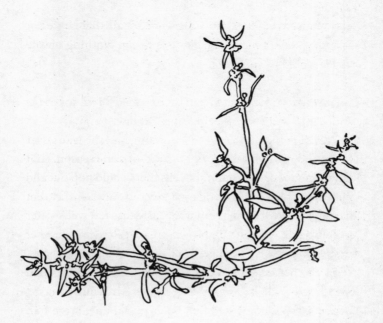

they're old. You can easily imagine that they made sense once but have hung around too long, have outlived their purpose and grown anachronistic, vestigial. And surely sometimes that's true. But if traditions are often strange, perhaps those acts and objects and stories and songs are traditional precisely *because* they are strange. Is it not the very strangeness, the unique curiosity of a thing, the arresting transformation or the essential contradiction of expectation that makes it worth sharing and repeating and passing along? Museums, I have said, are born of novelty. Indeed, they are borne upon it. They have no finer tradition. Yes, you eat—the first time— the corpse of a poisonous shark buried six months ago because you are starving. But you keep eating it, in a nation of plenty, because it is so eye-open stunning that such a thing can be done.

The Museum of the Story I Heard

The way I heard the story, it was a set designer. It was a man who had made his life in the theater: made risers and curtains and backdrops and trapdoors, made them transform a stage, made forests and sailing ships and utopias and apocalypses, made the future and the past. It was such a man, one who made liminal, unearthly spaces, made light and shadow tell a story.

Indeed it was *this* man, nearing the end of his career, who looked around and realized that for everything he had built, every staircase and tower and support and rig and river and night sky, there was nothing left to see. Everything had been torn down—all of it, by design, every last board—so that now, everything he had ever built had been unbuilt. All those worlds were gone. Everything he had made, perfectly, had been undone and unmade and disappeared.

In the face of all this nothingness, he made a museum instead.

I love this story. I love its elegance and its revolution. I love a problem neatly solved. I have heard this story from different sources, and on occasion I have heard it told about other museums. But I do not, ever, hear this story from him.

The story he tells is about the horseback trips, in the highlands, the groups he led with his wife in the summers. Even in these stories, he does not say everything. He does not talk about their favorite horses. He does not describe

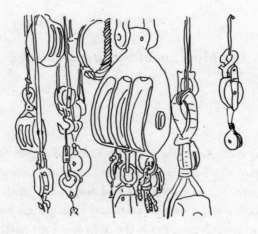

those wild places, the ancient tiny mosses, those windswept fragile blanks, the weather changing in an instant, the sideways rain and sleet-frozen hands. He talks about those long days riding, about how they told sagas to pass the time, to say something about the places they were passing through.

They told about the ugly son and the child dead on the ice and the sorceress queen and how poetry can save a man's life. They told these stories, and the riders loved them. The man and his wife wondered that their companions hadn't heard them before. These weren't even the obscure sagas. These were stories that survived for centuries, survived as canon and were celebrated, caused English literature PhDs of a certain era to learn Icelandic just to read them, and here they were unsaid and unknown. So they reached a conclusion. A museum. And then, together, they made a decision. They made plans, and they made choices, and they made a place to be walked through. They built a thing to be heard.

THE STONE

COLLECTOR

Petra's Stone Collection
(Steinasafn Petru)

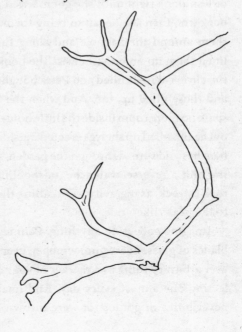

At first I felt as if I was borrowing the stones—but now I have come
to terms with the fact that they will remain here forever.

—LJÓSBJÖRG PETRA MARÍA SVEINSDÓTTIR

Almost every day of her life, Petra went for a walk.
Walks up into the hills mostly, but also walks along
the shore. Maybe walks along the relative flat of the un-
paved road hemming the eastern fjords, but mostly walks
with a vertical bent, a slope, walks with split and scrabble
and crag. And on almost every walk, they say, she found a
stone.

She didn't keep the stones. Not at first. Not for a long
time. She left them nestled in the hills or scattered among
the shells and the rocks and the shorebirds, left them more
or less alone right until she got married and had a place of
her own. Then she began to bring them home. She ringed
them around the flagpole and along the house wall. She
lined them up on bookshelves. The bookshelves filled and
the curio cabinets filled and Petra bought new bookshelves
and those filled up, too. And when the little family could
spare no more room inside the little home, the stones spilled
out again, filled up shelves erected outside and covered over
benches and spread through the garden, stretching back up
the hill: a reverse avalanche, unspooling in slow motion,
rock by rock, as if gravity were calling these stones back up
to the peaks like a tide.

Imagine collecting anything. Pennies or paper clips or
blades of grass. Every gum wrapper, every bus ticket, whatever arbitrary thing as a marker of your days. Imagine collecting one almost every day. And imagine these tokens
never broke or got lost or were thrown away. What a tre-

mendous lot of things. It would be a lot of tally marks, and it's certainly a lot of stones.

WHEN I SAY STONE, PERHAPS I SHOULD CLARIFY THAT I do not mean some plain-Jane piece of rock. I mean eye-catching. I mean white whisker-width spines radiating out in clusters like so many cowlicks. I mean a green between celery and mustard, pocked with pinprick bubbles and skimming like a rind over a vein that's crystal clear at the edges but clotting in the middle to the color of cream stirred into weak tea. I mean crystals like a jumble of molars and I mean jasper in oxblood and ocher and clover and sky, sometimes a hunk of one color but more likely a blend of two or three or five, maybe like ice creams melting together, or perhaps like cards stacked in a deck.

The eastern coast is the oldest part of Iceland, a crust of fourteen volcanoes, not all of them dead. All of Iceland has geological intrigue, including some 150 varieties of minerals, but the east seems particularly rich in both the frequency and variety with which the raw elements of the earth have been heated and pressed into wonders of color and texture and shape. It renders mint green and rouge red, flat matte and crystal clear, all of it spun in spindles and spires and lumps and swirls and brittles and pastes and bubbles and smears.

Jasper is particularly common to the east, but also onyx and opal and agate and amethyst. Fossils, too, though they're rarer. Up in Vopnafjörður they found the remains of a deer that arrived before the Ice Age. The fossilized deer is the only discovery of its kind, apparently from a place we would recognize now as Scotland, possibly crossed over on a land bridge long lost to us now.

*

IN THE BEGINNING, THEY SAY, PETRA WAS ALWAYS ALONE ON her walks. As a child she rambled with other children, but as a woman she walked alone. She spent hours in the hills instead of the home. People talked. It was not normal for a woman to be alone. They worried. It's not healthy to take the big rocks, they scolded. "Your back!" the neighbors fretted. "Your legs!"

The point was not necessarily solitude. At least, she was not always alone. There are stories of Petra out with her husband when he wasn't out on the boats, stories of the stones they left on the mountainside one day and found buried under an avalanche the next. There's the cavernous geode Petra and a friend discovered on the beach when they pulled over along a cove to find a sheltered place to pee. Those who went out with her say that everyone in the party could step over a spot, and then Petra would come to it and turn over a gem.

As Petra had her children, four all together, they packed themselves lunches and set out. The children could choose whether to go along, and sometimes they did and sometimes they didn't. After a while there were grandchildren following Petra into the hills, and great-grandchildren after that. Once Petra and her namesake granddaughter rolled a stone, too big to be lifted, all the way home. Once Petra and a friend set a fraction of their quarry by the road and went back for the rest, but when they returned to the road, the first cache was gone.

Petra reworked some flour sacks from her kitchen into bags for carrying the stones, and perhaps she considered the millstones that ground the flour in the first place, or perhaps she never gave it a thought. She might go to the mountains for six or seven or eight hours at a stretch. She might bring down a ninety-pound stone. Maybe she'd bring a toboggan or make a sleigh to move the weight. Maybe she'd return to the shore with a sweater to wrap the stone she'd found and a son to help and a washtub between them to lug it home.

Her ethics of stone collecting held that you couldn't damage anything to get at the piece you wanted, but you could go anywhere, and Petra might take you out to revisit a stone too big or too fragile or too stuck to take home. Even old paths reinvented themselves. Snow would fall or melt. Vegetation would bloom out or wither back. Things with claws or hooves would scratch or tunnel or kick up the dirt. The earth was certainly not creating new stones in a day, but in that same wink, erosion might reveal things differently than yesterday, a chance matter of water and wind and the persistent weak force pulling everything down.

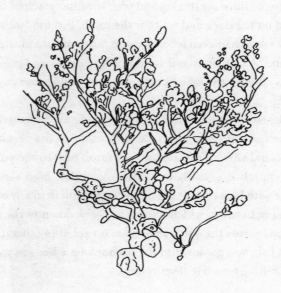

*

THE EAST IS THE SIDE OF THE COUNTRY WITH REINDEER. IT IS home to a lake monster in Lagarfljót and the elf queen in Álfaborg and 3 percent of all Icelanders. There are fjords and a fog that erases them. There are many stretches of sheep and cliffs. Most of the eastern towns are attached to harbors and are the kind of towns where there is probably a restaurant to feed you, should you stop in, but probably not two to choose from.

In Petra's town, Stöðvarfjörður, the café sells groceries, arranged in two aisles, each three strides long. In the refrigerator case you can buy a watermelon—not because Icelanders prize watermelons, but because importing the preponderance of your produce means apples are as exotic as mangoes, and why not have a star fruit if you can have a pear?

It is in Stöðvarfjörður that I learn you would never buy a fish. True, you have your fishmonger if you live in the capital, where the ships are too big and your time too precious to go stand on the dock and wait for the catch. But fish, substantially more than even wool sweaters, are a major industry in Iceland. And just as you would never buy a sweater—you know entirely too many knitters—you would never pay for a fish.

I learn this in a country church turned guesthouse where the red velvet pews now face each other in the breakfast nook, and where I'm sleeping on a futon next to the pulpit. The church is essentially a little box with a high steeple, white with blue trim. It sits higher up the hill than any other building in town, which affords it a view down to the harbor and across the fjord. The owner is explaining that if you want fish, you go down to the harbor where her son works on a fishing boat. He'll set you up.

"How will I know which boat is his?" I ask.

"Doesn't matter," she says. Because you can ask any boat. Because a boat comes in with its catch and you wave to the fishermen and you shout that you want to buy a fish. Who knows if they even hear you? But they see you and they look around the decks and they pick a fish and they throw it into your arms.

"How much?" you might call out, your hands full of scales. But they don't want your money. They wave you off. What, would you toss your kronur to them? Pay for your catch with silver lumpfish and shore crabs and capelins stamped on shining coins? It's small change anyway, and they'll give you only a small fish—a fish longer than any bone in your arm, to be sure, but those are the runts.

Stöðvarfjörður had 380 inhabitants when the fish factory was in full swing. For many years Petra was one of the workers cleaning and deboning the fish there, her husband one of the fishermen hauling them in. These days it's a town of two hundred, struggling to keep a school closure at bay. The residents are enterprising and obliging and hoping someone, a few someones, will move in and have some kids.

IN THE BEGINNING, IT FELT TO PETRA LIKE A MONOPOLY. SHE was born in 1922 and married in 1945 and the following year moved to a house called Sunnuhlíð, for its situation on a sunny slope. For the next twenty years, it seemed she had the hills more or less to herself. Her favorite mountains were Steðjinn and Ólukkan, the Anvil and Misfortune, though who could deny the charm of Sauðdalur, the Valley of the Sheep?

For twenty years she ranged between the shore and the slope and the mountains north of town. For twenty years she worked in the fish factory and raised her children and looked after her mother-in-law. Sunnuhlíð was filled and bordered and ringed with stones. It was filled with three children in one tiny room, Petra and her husband in another, and the mother-in-law alone in the last. For twenty years Petra emptied her bags on the kitchen table, and her children asked if they were getting rocks for supper.

There was one road then, as there is one road now, but the one road then stopped at the south edge of town. Just stopped. Fizzled out and kaput, nowhere left to go that a boat or a horse could not traverse better. In 1962 the road was extended and made sturdy enough for motor vehicles to travel south out of town. The road meant Petra began to stir farther afield, beyond the shore and the slope, beyond the Anvil and Misfortune. But the more profound effect was not of Petra going out, but of travelers coming in.

They say foreigners came to collect stones long before the Icelanders themselves took an interest. They came with marked-up maps and pneumatic drills and pressure cylinders and candy to give the kids. Germans, they say, came early and come still. Ferry passengers returned to mainland Europe, pockets full of obsidian, so smooth and so sharp.

IF YOU WERE LOOKING FOR SOMETHING TO COLLECT, NOT that any collection begins so sensibly, but if you were thinking of ideal collectibles, you wouldn't be wrong to pick something hardy. No finicky temperature or humidity requirements, no delicate parts at risk with every dusting. Ideally, you'd want a thing that could forgo even the secondary upkeep of shelter, a thing inclined to weather the outdoors with no special preservation. And if those somethings happened to be free for the taking, your collecting would be limited only by the fortune to find them and the effort to get them home.

I sometimes think the twin attractions of Petra's stone collection are the plainly extraordinary and the terrifically familiar. It's not just the volume and quality and sheer fact of so much chalcedony and spar existing at all, let alone in one place. We marvel at this singular woman, Sisyphus reversed, admire her independence and diligence and taste. We kneel here at this museum of her commitment, at its altar of daily ritual, awed at its yield, even as we suspect in our secret hearts that we, too, could have done it. We've been known to walk up a beautiful hill. We know enough to bend when something shines and beckons. If only we'd had the time or were born in such a conducive landscape or if any little variable of history or circumstance shifted ever so slightly, surely we would have done the very same thing. Perhaps Petra reminds us of what we already suspect: that the world is chockablock with untold wonders, there for the taking, ready to be uncovered at any moment if only we keep our eyes open. We flatter ourselves that we are Petra. *We* wouldn't countenance the naysayers. *We* wouldn't fear the storms that come up in an instant. No, we would follow our desires, our simple pleasures, our benign passions, and make something astonishing without even meaning to. Maybe we already have and just haven't noticed yet. Maybe we'll start tomorrow.

Precisely because the stones can be stored outside on the ground, Petra could collect as many as the long narrow lot would hold. And partly because people talked, but mostly because they could see the pooling aggregate of stones from the side of the road, they stopped to look. And once they stopped to look, they started to come closer. And once they'd come closer, they asked to come inside.

PETRA'S KITCHEN IS YOUR GRANDMOTHER'S KITCHEN. THE mauve cabinet doors and the pistachio paint. The rack of dishes on display, and an abundance of tea sets and drinking glasses and mugs.

With the kitchen table pushed to the wall, there's seating for five, though the guides coming in and out often stand. The way the table abuts the wall, it puts a roof over the heater's grate, and heat collects under the tabletop, trapped by the tablecloth's hem, so that when you're sitting at her table, your thighs can be toasty and your feet still cold. A clear plastic tablecloth protects fifteen lace doilies, patterned like flowers and snowflakes, made by the woman herself.

The centerpiece is a glass cake dome, filled today with sandwiches cut into little pieces, and flanked by a brass serving dish full of teaspoons.

A bus driver eating a slice of cake says Petra once gave him a stone. His daughter sleeps with it under her pillow. Petra would do this, give you a stone for yourself or someone close to you or for some special purpose. Early on she gave stones to the Icelandic Museum of Natural History in Reykjavík, but they kept her stones in a box in storage somewhere, and Petra gave up sending them anything.

The kitchen was always like this. Not just the decor of straw dolls and needlepoint and rings of keys and bottle openers, but also the eddy of family and tour guides and bus drivers and stray visitors wandering in.

"Part of this house was having strangers in it." That's what Þórkatla says. She's the youngest of Petra's four children. There's a seventeen-year spread from first to last. The third child, Sveinn, built a house two doors down, after he petitioned the president to be allowed to marry a year earlier than the legislated minimum age of eighteen. Sveinn and his bride are married still, and they never moved away. He polishes the stones, and she makes jewelry for the gift shop, but then all of the children contribute. The second-oldest child, Elsa Lísa, also lives in town, while Ingimar and Þórkatla both come for a stretch every summer.

Each of the children remembers the strangers. Ingimar recalls returning home one day as a kid and discovering five tourists in the garden. Sveinn says there were always visitors about. Elsa Lísa remarks how the family never closed its door to people who wanted inside. Sitting around the kitchen table now, all of Petra's children nod their heads. Yes, that's how it was: You'd come home and you'd come home to strangers.

HENRI IS A FRENCHMAN WITH WILD GRAY CURLS AND THE glint of a tiny gold hoop in his ear. He can't remember when he started bringing tours to see the stones, but it's been some decades. He notes that every year the place is a little more organized, the garden a little finer. I ask Henri what other stops he makes on his tour, what comes before this and what comes after. "This is it," he says. "This is the stop in the east fjords."

Laufey is an art historian who has been guiding here for forty years. Forty years of forty-five-minute stops. Forty years taking her break in this kitchen, drinking coffee from these cups. She remembers the professional geologists who came seeking advice. She remembers Petra "could tell a story about every stone." Once she invited Petra to visit her in Paris, and Petra did, and became "The only person I've had in Paris who found a stone in Paris."

You might expect a certain competition Among tour guides, some sort of territory to protect. But guide after guide assures me, as they rotate through Petra's kitchen, that the way it was then is the way it is now: If you found a place worth stopping for, you shared it. Maybe you stumble on something during a lunch break, maybe you note something in an article, probably it's word of mouth. Laufey is earnest on this point of etiquette: "Among the guides, we tell each other the good places."

Their influence was expansive. It was the guides who started bringing busloads of people to see the stones. It was the guides who started telling Petra to charge admission, though she refused. It was the guides who made the private garden of a private home the one and only point of interest in all the east fjords.

"When the tours started, we had to ask Petra if it was okay," Laufey says. And because Petra said yes, kept saying yes, always said yes, the guides filled up coaches, filled them with cruise-ship passengers and package tours and tourists signed up for a day trip, and brought them all to the garden to walk through her yard.

PETRA'S BEDROOM LOOKS LIKE THE BED WAS MADE THIS morning, though it's been uninhabited for a few years now. Everything seems ready to be returned to: a slender TV stand, a handful of bobbins and reading glasses, a poster of the national handball team. It's the kind of modest room where one can stand in the center and touch both long walls at the same time, with one hand landing in a shelf of books that cantilevers over the narrow bed. On that shelf, alongside six volumes of Jón Árnason's history of Iceland and bound collections of *Tíminn* periodicals from 1962 to 1979, sit four linear feet worth of guest books.

The guest books begin a few years after the road in town was made to go through—after the strangers started to appear in the garden but before the guides arrived.

Guest Book I has a blue cover with gold lettering and spans the years 1966 to 1973. The first day on record is August 16, and it logs the visit of two people: Sölvi Ólason and Margrét Sveinsdóttir—the husband of Petra's cousin Kristin, and Petra's sister, respectively. The next day Margrét's husband writes his name. The day after it's a friend who lived in the blue-and-white house three doors down. Two days later, five people sign in, and three days later there are five more. "This," a granddaughter says to me, pointing to an entry with a laugh of surprise, "this is my mother's best friend and *her* mother."

In the beginning, even inhabitants of the house on the sunny slope tallied themselves in its guest book. On page three of Guest Book I, then-five-year-old Þórkatla and her older sister Elsa Lísa write their names. Two years later, seven-year-old Þórkatla inserts herself again. Perhaps they were bored. Perhaps they sometimes felt they, too, were visitors. By 1972 the guest book is six years old and documents visitors from Denmark and two of Iceland's northern cities, Akureyri and Húsavík. By 2000, in a much later guest book, a party records itself with one name and the summary "+ 30 Italians."

NO ONE REMEMBERS WHETHER THE TOUR GUIDES OR THE journalists came first. Perhaps it doesn't matter. Perhaps it was a tie. The first newspaper clipping saved in the guest books advertises the 1969 Hitchcock movie *Topaz* on one side—a movie *in color*, the ad notes. The other side features two paragraphs under a headline that translates as "Stone Collection & Mountain Walk." At the end of the two paragraphs, there is no period. There is no jump to the next page. Surely the article was longer, but the clipping ends mid-sentence, suddenly, like a cliff.

IN THE OLD DAYS IN ICELAND, TRAVELERS WENT BY FOOT OR by horse. The going was slow and the weather could be deadly, so when they found a farmhouse, they could pretty well count on the offer of accommodation for the night. Not just shelter and a meal, even, but the likelihood of being sent on with a picnic lunch and a new pair of shoes. Shoes were made of fishskin or maybe sealskin and could be cut to ribbons in a day's walk, such that distances were sometimes measured in the number of shoes you'd need to cross them. It was common decency to take travelers in, to spare them from frostbite or exposure or just freezing to death. But hosting had another incentive, travelers being quite possibly the only news source and novelty you might get for weeks, at least until the next one happened into your valley, or you had to go journey somewhere yourself.

I think about this historic hospitality, about how a private place becomes public by degrees, about how the distinction becomes fuzzy from the get-go. It wasn't just that Petra allowed visitors into her garden, or that she then invited them into her kitchen for a cup of coffee and some cake. She might invite a trio of weary Americans to stay for supper. Or a storm would come through and she'd put up a dozen Italian cyclists stranded for the night.

For a long time the museum was not a museum. Not

officially. It was a private home with a private garden that happened to attract tour guides and journalists and strangers off the road. And then one day, in 1974, Petra was traveling in Denmark with her husband—they had waited so long to start making such trips—when his heart gave out and he died. The family decided at his funeral that it was time to make a museum. Everyone just seemed to know. Even now the family talks about how they make all the museum's decisions together. They talk about how they've never disagreed. They say that together, that night of the funeral—instantly, unanimously—they decided it was time to open the gates to the public. Though, of course, the gates were already open. The public was already there.

ARGUABLY, THE TURNING POINT CAME EARLIER. ONE DAY Petra met a tourist in the hallway of her home. The tourist asked for directions to the bathroom. Petra pointed and the tourist said that it was already occupied. The tourist asked for directions to another, and Petra explained that there was just the one. The tourist then demanded to know, "What kind of museum has only one bathroom?" A good question, of course. Except that it wasn't a museum back then. It was a house with facilities totally adequate for the three people who actually lived there.

The joke in the family is that Petra would collect anything except money or clothes. No one told her to start wearing makeup or expand her wardrobe beyond functional shoes and her favorite red vest, but the guides were forever telling her to charge admission and she was forever telling them no. Maybe she didn't believe she owned the rocks in the first place. Maybe it tempts fate to put a price on joy. But the toilet brought things to a head.

Aslaug, a guide who splits her time between Iceland and France, has been bringing tours to Petra's since the 1970s, since the one-toilet days. She is clear on this point: "Toilet is very important when you are a guide." And maybe this is the structure of all museums. One doesn't pay to see the collection; one pays for a place to pee.

THE STONES DON'T CHANGE. IT'S THE NEEDS OF THE visitors that drive expansion. By 1989 there was a small entrance fee, to pay for the toilets, three of them eventually, all still in service in a little hut off the garden. That same year Petra decided to retire from the fish factory, to stop slicing and skinning and prepping the catch. She might instead escort a group of children down to the shore, the party returning to empty their buckets onto her kitchen floor, the better to examine the sand and the shells and whatever twitching feeling parts sometimes extended from their rattled casings.

After the toilets came the sun porch addition to the side of the house, with couches and plants, and glassed in like a greenhouse. Then the family made a book you can buy in the gift shop. Around the year 2000 they added a ticket booth to the property (before that there had been a mailbox down the road where you could donate some money if you wanted). And just in 2015, they added a coffeehouse. Maybe they'll add Wi-Fi next, maybe update the website. Maybe it's time to produce a self-guided tour.

It's a great-grandson of Petra's, a teenager with floppy blond hair and a beaming smile, who's now in the ticket booth selling you your tickets. It's his summer job before he heads home to Reykjavík. There's a granddaughter and a great-granddaughter inside the house, behind the gift shop counter. The great-granddaughter is turning twenty-two today, so there is a birthday cake in the kitchen: an inch of yellow cake supporting an inch of chocolate frosting thick enough to submerge slices of canned pears. A woman brings doughnuts cut in quarters. The birthday girl herself produces a blueberry cheesecake, and when that has been consumed her aunt replaces it with its twin.

Petra has thirteen grandchildren. There are plenty of great-grands, but her four kids agree it's too much trouble to count them all. Not one of Petra's heirs has become a geologist by profession, but the clan gathers every Easter to start cleaning the stones, every stone inside the house and every stone spread up the sunny slope, preparing the garden for tourist season, though there will be snow through the middle of May. If they're lucky, there's been a lot of snow, enough to act like a blanket, tamping things down, packing them snug until spring. But whatever the winter has wrought, there will always be benches to mend, stones to rearrange. The bulbs planted last fall will begin to bloom.

WHEN PETRA WAS A CHILD, THE STREAMS HAD TROUT ENOUGH to catch with your friends and bring back to a waiting tub, where you could feed the fish insects and endeavor to teach them tricks. There is no museum of trout tricks. You'd be lucky now to find even the tubs.

When Petra was a girl, she knew another girl, Rósalinda. Maybe Petra thought Rósa was mean. Maybe Rósa thought Petra was boring. But over time, they reconsidered. There is a photograph of them together, teenagers in dresses of their own making, cut from the same cloth. They were friends the rest of their lives.

They say Petra and Rósa were eight or nine when they shook hands and agreed to always give each other a birthday present, even in the event of discord—a handkerchief, at the very least. This went on until Rósa was old and could not travel, entrusting her children to ferry the handkerchiefs to Petra. And when Petra was in much the same state, her children were charged with taking handkerchiefs to Rósa. There is no museum of their exchange. There is no museum for a lot of things. But a selection of the tokens Rósa sent and Petra kept is on display in a little enclosure in the garden called the Storyhouse, the napkins smooth and pressed and tucked between Petra's collection of seashells and her collection of matchbooks.

I always loved working in museums. I loved the whole project of it. Here we were, in the business of making the material and intellectual history of the world available to anyone who so much as came looking. How generous! How righteous! How good! But the more I paid attention, the stranger it seemed. Here we were, limited in the first place to the preservation of those things that *can* be kept. Who could know all that was already lost? How much has become unknown or unknowable simply because it is no longer there to be counted?

Add to that another filter: What we do have, the existing collections we have to choose from, are thanks to a handful of self-selected volunteers. There is no systematic attempt to cover the board. Already we cannot hold on to all the things we think are worthwhile, much less those things we would need to keep long enough to reconsider. We work from the whim of collectors—how is this not shortsighted and haphazard?

You might be obsessed with Elvis or the Alamo or scarecrows or snowflakes or any of the marvels and novelties and iterations of the world. It almost doesn't matter which, because the collector's master passion is so often not the ostensible subject of a collection, but the very act of *collecting*. Indeed, if you're free to look, you will find that a collector tends to collect all sorts of things—one single collector

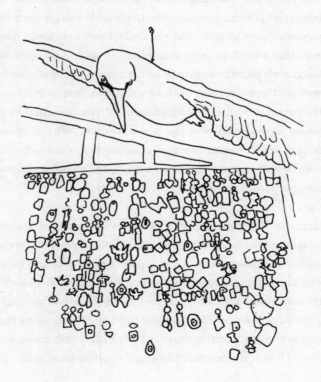

may be obsessed with antique automobiles and pipe organs and hood ornaments and musical instruments that play themselves. Yet, at best, one, maybe two of those collections will achieve any particular recognition, with the rest of that collecting eclipsed.

Certainly it wasn't just stones. Petra collected pens and lighters and coasters and playing cards and postcards and key chains, though no one recommends you make the trip to see just them. Petra's stone collection is what it is partly because she made it and partly because thousands more made it known.

Yes, collectors collect. We need them to do that. But it's something else that makes museums. With every visit and article and affirming word, collectively and by degree, whole groups of people select for the collections *they* fancy, the ones that somehow have something to add. And with silence, with indifference, they select against the rest. Museums are the expression of those collective determinations. They are rooted in a network of cooperative affirmation long before anyone whispers the word *museum*. What a quiet democracy. What an enormous collaboration at work. No wonder this curious family of organisms, these museums emerging from our gaze.

THE EAST FOG IS IN TODAY. IT RENDERS THE MOUNTAINTOPS erased and the land across the fjord almost invisible. I walk toward the museum, watch it appear and recede, and keep walking past, southeast on the one road going anywhere. There is a cemetery with a white fence and a white gate just at the edge of town. The sidewalk ends, and I walk along the side of the road, noting from the flecks and glimmers and crystal bits at my feet that the gravel must be local stone.

When I decide to walk Petra's hills, there are no trails to guide me. Not Petra's, not anyone's. The ground is covered thickly in a spongy green vegetation that both cushions the joints and obscures the terrain such that I step with a bounce but without knowing how deep my foot will fall before finding purchase. The loamy mantle springs back without registering any mark of my path, and I would worry about losing my way except that on this steep slope there is no confusing the cardinal directions of uphill and down.

One of Petra's granddaughters, Kristjana, says that to go rock hunting you look for the streams, the places where the rock is exposed. She says that water will reveal land. Streams are easy enough to find. In half a mile I have my pick of them, as the water cuts ever more paths flowing to the sea. A black-and-white bird with intensely orange beak and feet cries out and circles, and I wish I knew where the nest was so I could avoid it more scrupulously. There are flowers, thin and tiny and what I would call delicate except they survive in a place that can be so harshly cold and dark.

At first I see nothing more notable than the occasional glitter of the gravel. Then I find little pockets and lines of champagne-colored crystals that break off in my hands. A rare stretch of rock face bares vertical puddles of frosted blue stone set in the slate-gray sheet, none of it yielding.

I had thought the tricky part would be finding anything special at all. I figured the odds weren't promising in the first place, and I was too green to spot the good stuff anyway. I have picked up rocks wherever I've walked, admiring creek stones and beach stones that dried to nothing special. I know those glossy nuggets in rock shops like nothing

I've seen in the deserts they come from. For the most part, the world's landscapes have taught me that besides a little quartz, a few flecks of fool's gold, the prizes tend to be as unassuming as geodes: essentially unremarkable until the intervention of a cut or a polish or an expert eye.

But I wasn't in Petra's hills one afternoon before I saw that the trick had nothing to do with the odds of encounter. It wasn't a matter of equipment, and it had nothing to do with opening my eyes or my heart or whatever. This was more of a Goldilocks proposition, merely a matter of the patience to find a stone neither too big nor too small. This was only waiting to choose the thing worth holding on to, the thing worth taking home.

A LITTLE GIRL IN THE GIFT SHOP FUMBLES WITH A ZIPPERED pocket and a clatter of flat platter stones until she can pinch out the one she found yesterday at the beach. Her mother explains with a British accent how the little girl knew they were coming here today and she wanted to ask about this one. Þórkatla tells her what it's called, walks it behind the counter, and the girl rises on her tiptoes to follow the rock as it disappears in Þórkatla's hand and then bobs back up in a plastic bag with a paper tag announcing its type. "It's a special rock," the mother says to the little girl. "So special it has a name."

Until recently, most of Iceland's museums opened only for summer traffic. The same was true for most lodging and restaurants and even certain roads. A lot of bus service still shuts down, and a whole chain of hotels operates out of schools closed for summer break. That Petra's stone collection became a museum at all was because the stones were outside, where they could be seen; for exactly the same reason, it remains limited to a seasonal attraction.

The summer is still plenty busy. At last count, some twenty-five thousand visitors come each summer, between the first good days in May and some point in late August or early September—depending on the weather, and the crowds—when the family hosts what they call Josar Naut, Light Evening. It is a kind of thank-you to neighbors and friends, in which the family fills the garden with candles, invites an accordionist to play, and serves coffee and kleinur and pancakes. Imagine everyone full and content, nestled among the stones, all of it illuminated from a hundred points of flicker and glow. The music drifts up the slope and down to the shore and out of town on the one road going anywhere.

If you ask how many stones there are in Petra's collection, no one has bothered to do a tally. Not Petra, not anyone. Sometimes the suggestion is made to occupy energetic children: "Why don't you go count the stones?" But even the kids who start soon discover it's so much better to run through the garden, race its looping paths. Why count stones when there's the chance to frighten a little bird or discover a gnome or risk tipping into a decorative pond?

Whatever they say, though, about children beyond counting, about all those would-be witnesses and surveyors grown daunted or distracted, I like to think some irrepressible soul, some someone somewhere, did it once: carried out the census scrupulously. Not that it matters, the number of stones. The sum does precious little to explain this place. It does not account for an accidental monument built stone by stone. It does not justify the collection of people drawn to it decade after decade. It gives us nothing new.

I started counting the stones once, but I'm not the one to tell you a figure for their sum. I don't mind that. I want only to be assured that such a person does indeed exist. I want to know, to believe, that just such a person is walking among us—close, I hope—holding a secret it seems anyone at all could arrive at, yet no one else knows.

The Museum of What Is Real

I keep staring at the wounded limb, mesmerized: the way it's cradled by the other arm, the faux blood so bright and already spreading through the gauze. This mannequin is the worst off of all the mannequins waiting in line, and yet it is surely still better off than the bedridden one in a dim open-walled room adjacent, however tenderly that patient is ministered to by a doting mannequin nun.

I cannot remember what these injured bodies have to do with French fishermen in Iceland, whether their infirmary is meant to be in their home country or if it is the reason to come ashore here. Perhaps I am distracted. Certainly, I cannot keep from mind that the women in France who married these sailors were known as the widows of Iceland—the work so dangerous that the wives were called widows before their husbands even died.

The story is well told. The museum is thoughtful and well-appointed and freshly painted. I cannot believe how effective the fancy new interactive tables are, every chapter so engaging, the technology so state-of-the-art. These portals tell how the sailors stocked up on salt in Portugal and cheap wine in Spain. That the canvas sails made the fjords look like forest. That each fish was counted aloud, so precious, and their enumeration so regular, so close to shore, that even the Icelandic locals could count fluently in French. There is something crisp and beautiful even in the triage queue tableau, though I can't imagine how this posh hotel came to put a museum in the lobby, a glimpse of old suffering on the way to check-in.

There is more, if you seek it out, if you follow the signs. Downstairs one descends to a ship. The floor sways like the ocean. The view projected on the wall is of waves bobbing into whitecaps—except the white parts are names, forming and unforming, the names of all the French fishermen lost in Icelandic waters, now recalled as peak and froth, if you sway long enough. If you need to stand still, you step from the ship deck into the bunk room, into the discomfort of tight quarters, the mannequins sleeping cramped, fitfully it seems, crumpled in their beds.

Everything downstairs smells like fish. And like salt. Not altogether unlike low tide. I am surprised that this hotel has been so committed, has welcomed history right down to the stench. I wonder if it comes out from the old ship boards, from the genuine old deck reassembled here. I wonder if they pump it in.

I ask the person on staff at the museum desk. She is neither French nor Icelandic, but a Polish landscape architect here because there is work at the aluminum-smelting plant, because the energy is so cheap it's worth shipping the metal here from mines in Brazil. I ask her about the fish smell, about how they manage it so well.

"Visitors," she says.

When the museum opened two months ago, at the cusp of summer, they had set up the ship's deck the way it would have been: real fish really curing in real barrels of real salt. It's the old way of doing things, the way it would have been.

"But the visitors," she says. "They kept picking up the fish."

The visitors would pinch a tail and raise it up, the slumped body like a weight, the nose dangling just above the pack of salt. The visitors would inspect its scales, heft its mass, consider the feel between their fingers, and decide it was in fact real. It seems that's what they wondered in the midst of memorial: Is this fish real?

Because they kept pulling the fish from the salt, interrupting the chemistry at work, the fish didn't cure as it should have, as it always had on real boats. From all that handling, all that disruption, all that checking to make sure, the fish began to go bad. The fish was real in the ocean and real in the salt and now it was really decomposing—until the museum had to send someone down to pick it up on purpose, officially, to pluck the breaking-down fish from the now slippery salt. It will not be replaced.

I ask how long since they had to throw out the aromatic fish.

"It's been six weeks," she says.

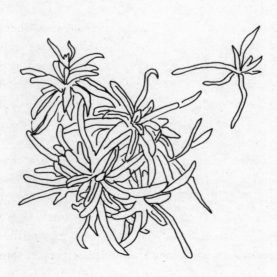

I'm not sure what's more amazing—that such a bouquet was created so quickly, or that it so pungently persists. I admire its reality, its presence, though its source is utterly intangible now.

Of course the museum could not keep the stinking fish. Everything forbids it. I imagine its removal in cartoon: by a schoolmarm, strict and stern, saying something about *the rules*, the children shamed but disappointed as they wail to have it back. And this is how it always is with the public, with museums, with the best-laid plans. A thing is met with priceless curiosity, and from that engagement transformed.

VAGRANTS AND

UNCOMMON

VISITORS

Sigurgeir's Bird Museum
(*Fuglasafn Sigurgeirs*)

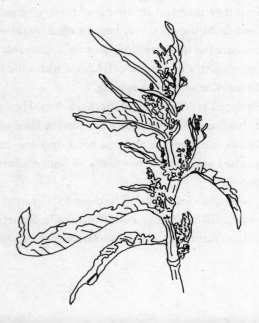

Their grandmother was blind. She hadn't always been, but as the glaucoma took her sight, she would ask, each day, what birds were on the water. The farm where they lived was on a shoreline, a piece of land poking into the great wide lake. Half the year the lake froze over, and sometimes mist blew through or clouds of midges swarmed up, but every day she asked and every day they told her. There might be twenty or more species to report in a given day. The short-eared owl and the long-tailed duck. The red-throated loon or the black-headed gull, the Barrow's golden-eye or the purple sandpiper, the common redshank or the ruddy turnstone. And any of the kids might answer, but probably it was Sigurgeir, Sigurgeir especially, who would be the one to tell her.

The family farm had been settled in 1888. It's called Ytri-Neslöndum, meaning "northern peninsula," named for its position on the lake, and it remains one of Lake Mývatn's two dozen traditional farms. It has a house and a cowshed and a smoke shed and another shed for drying either laundry or fish, as the need may be, and what might once have been a barn but is now nothing short of a mechanic's garage, complete with a pinup-girl calendar, a hydraulic lift, and a '74 Monte Carlo that needs work.

Sigurgeir was born on the farm in 1962. He was one of three brothers and four sisters, here on the farm with sheep and cows and chickens and one horse and one dog and always a bed of rhubarb. They made an honest effort to grow potatoes.

These seven kids, like all farmers' kids around the lake, grew up collecting eggs, collecting shells. Sigurgeir had a friend one farm over, and they went collecting together. As

you collected eggs, you'd trade them, like baseball cards—
your divers for their shorebirds.

The rule of collecting eggs is a Solomon-simple even
split: You take half. Half for you and half for the nest. You
could take fewer, I suppose, but whatever you do, there is
a threshold. The rule at Ytri-Neslöndum was never leave
fewer than four eggs in a nest. Other places it was never
fewer than five, or six, depending on which species owned
the nest. If you're taking from a horned grebe nest, you
might leave a single egg, knowing, as you do, how the first
to hatch will be the only one to survive. And if you're struggling with the math of survival, wondering how one arrives
at any minimum number as the standard of husbandry,
consider that there is an upper limit, too. The birds themselves can't manage more than a certain number, after all;
they simply can't warm any more than what's snugged in
the down of their bird bodies.

You pull eggs from different species at different times.
Each has its own clock. Still, the whole of egg collecting
lasts not much longer than one month a year. It ends, of
course, when there are not eggs but goslings and cygnets
and whatever you call baby black-tailed godwits. But it begins, by one reckoning, when you mix chalk in water, and if
a potato floats, then it's time to take the eggs.

For a while, then, it's eggs for baking and eggs for om-
elets, eggs for as long as they last. Eggs dipped in chalk or ash
at the smokehouse. They say each species of egg tastes different, the ducks different from the grebes. But no matter their
flavor, all of them look the same split from their shells—
different in scale, perhaps, more or less albumen, but always
those intense dark yolks like tiny orange suns.

*

LAKE MÝVATN IS FULL OF LIFE. EXCESSIVELY, ABUNDANTLY
so. Eutrophic, as the scientists say. It is named for the midges
that swarm prodigiously in summer, thickly, like weather,
trapped buzzing in your hair or else their bodies wet lumps
stuck to the back of your throat or lodged irretrievably up
your nostrils or caught in your eye and eventually blinked
out like a black tear.

In the far east of the country there are signs in the bath-
rooms announcing, "We do not have geothermal heat—
please use hot water sparingly." By the time you arrive some
hours later at Mývatn, in the northeastern quadrant of the
country and about as far inland as you may venture without
tackling the Highlands, your approach has been marked by a
succession of wide rivers and waterfalls and eventually cracks
in the earth venting steam. In Mývatn you go to turn on the
tap and someone suggests, in light of the sulfur so commonly
companion to the geothermic water supply, "Maybe use
the cold, or else the water will have a smell."

Spring water feeds the lake, and the nutrients in the
spring water feed a bounty of aquatic insects—notably the
midges—and the insects feed whatever will swallow them
down, most notably the ducks. The visitor center announces,
"Nowhere in the world are there so many species of duck in
the same place." For the record, that makes fourteen the
number to beat, or some years fifteen, but in any case it's all
the duck species that appear in Iceland minus the two species spotted strictly on the coast. There are both Eurasian
and North American ducks here, as well as arctic species
and boreal. There are dabbling ducks and diving ducks—
not to mention fifteen hundred pairs of Eurasian wigeon.

And there's the horned grebe, too, a red-eyed migrator

that breeds in Iceland. The bird makes a floating nest of rotting marsh and tethers it to surrounding plants, that it may
rise and fall with the current but not be swept away.

WHEN SIGURGEIR TURNED SEVENTEEN, HE GOT A DRIVER'S
license and a car, a blue Mitsubishi Lancer, what an old
friend still remembers as "a very strong, good car." He was
the kind of guy who would give you a lift, so you'd call him.
It can be hard to get around the wetlands, but there he was,
so affable, and he would drive 95 miles for a dance without
thinking about it. He'd make a couple of trips to get everyone there, if that's what it took.

There is no national dance in Iceland. It's just not a form
of expression, perhaps because dances were outlawed for a
time a few centuries back, legislated away in a society where
it was understood you couldn't get married unless you had
enough money. And so certain people married late or not at
all, but the thing about dances was that they brought people
together and you ended up with babies whether everyone
was married or not. And so, from the twelfth century to
the seventeenth, it was just safer not to dance. Not that the
babies stopped. Not that the young people at Sigurgeir's
dances would have danced a national dance had they had
one—not when there was Michael Jackson.

Things change, of course.

Waxwings never used to be in Iceland at all, but now
they're laying here. The tufted duck, one of the divers, only
came to Iceland at the end of the nineteenth century and is
now the most common duck species to be found.

WHEN SIGURGEIR WAS TWENTY, A GREY HERON, A BIRD
foreign to Iceland, was discovered one farm over. The farmer

found it, dead. It happens from time to time, a non-native arrival, happens not just here but anywhere. Birds are caught up in storms, blown out to sea, pulled by a current and washed up on the wrong shore. Though perhaps it's not always some external, unaccountable intervention. Or at least maybe, sometimes, it is no one thing alone that sheers a few individuals away from the territory they know, sends them on their eccentric orbit, away from the rest of the flock.

In the language of ornithology, birds are classed by their abundance in five descending steps: common, less common, uncommon, rare, and vagrant. The first four classes have to do with certainty, with whether you can absolutely depend on seeing a bird in suitable habitat and proper season, or whether you might have to wait two or five years between sightings. But vagrants are rarer than rare. Vagrants are out of their normal range; they have appeared somewhere new. Which is to say, you may have common migrants or uncommon visitors and to some degree predict their comings and goings. But vagrants are so unusual, there is no reason to expect them at all.

The farmer put the heron in the freezer. Perhaps because he was waiting. Perhaps because something irrecoverable had happened and now he did not know what to do. Perhaps because there was room in the freezer and all the time in the world. I assume he folded the legs like you would collapse an umbrella, folded the beak to the neck and the neck to the body. One day, when Sigurgeir was at that neighbor's farm, the farmer showed the bird to him. What was there to say?

The farmer made a gift of the vagrant bird that had no precedent, that shouldn't have been there in the first place. Sigurgeir accepted the frozen four pounds, five maybe, and took the heron to a taxidermist on the seacoast, in Dalvík. This was his first stuffed bird. If a collection is a colony, that is how this one began.

WHEN EVERYONE COMES HOME IN THE SUMMER, FOUR hundred people live around Lake Mývatn. Half that stay year-round. That's not unusually small as Icelandic towns go—pretty average, really—and even though this population is spread out, on a lakeside loop well suited to the marathon staged here once a year, it is still a town too small for secrets. Which is to say, when you come to take an interest in dead birds, it will be known. You will start to get calls from all around the lake, first from the neighbors, but then from anyone, whenever there is something you really should come see.

WHEN SIGURGEIR RETURNED TO DALVÍK FOR THE GREY heron, that bird that should never have been on this island, he was moved to purchase two more birds from the taxidermist's shop: a puffin and a northern fulmar.

The northern fulmar looks like a snub-nosed seagull, the head clean white, as if that was the part you held on to while dip-dyeing the rest of the bird in washes of weak gray ink. Two hundred fifty years ago, the only known colony of northern fulmars in the whole Atlantic was here in northern Iceland. Now there are hundreds of colonies, thousands of birds, not just here but also off the Faeroe Islands and British Isles. They are absolutely abundant in the subarctic, the species now spread so far and wide perhaps because this relative of the albatross knows so cunningly how to scavenge the scraps from fishing boats and whaling ships plowing the northern Atlantic waves. It is a bird shaped like a gull, though it glides like a shearwater. Only one confirmed sighting has ever put it in the Southern Hemisphere. It begins breeding "at an exceptionally old age," but perhaps that is only because it is one of the longest-lived birds we know.

A puffin is a bird built like a bullet. Even its wings are compact, look dense for all their feathers and hollow bones. Its feet are safety-cone orange, its face painted in harlequin surprise, a bird that never stops flapping its wings in flight, never glides or soars, but beats frantically, unceasingly, its expression a constant shock that any of this is working out at all. But all these concessions of flight so that it might dive. It dives deep and plunging, tracing sharp down-up V shapes and wide-troughed U's and wily, wandering, double-dip W's. It surfaces with fish that hang out of its beak like silver mustaches, a flop fluttering fringe. But when the taxidermists pose them, they neither dive nor swim nor madly beat their wings. They stand on rocks, looking down at their feet with an air of bewilderment, or staring at the horizon, beaks lifted, their bearing almost noble.

The northern fulmar is among the most common species to be found on Iceland's coasts, but the puffin is represented so widely in shops catering to tourists that the Icelanders call these mercantiles "puffin shops." When Sigurgeir selected the puffin and the northern fulmar to take home with the grey heron, he mixed the coastal with the inland, the common with the vagrant. And in picking this pairing of Icelandic icons, he matched an unwitting pair of complements. If the puffin is a study in high contrast, the northern fulmar is all gray-scale gradation. If the puffin is struggle and drop, the northern fulmar is fluid and glide. And if the northern fulmar represents the prosperity of

prodigious expansion, the puffin, I am sorry to report, suggests something shifting and uncertain.

If you had grown up on the opposite side of the island, in
Heimaey, on the only inhabited island in the Vestmannaeyjar island chain off the southwest coast, you would have
had an August ritual. You would have gone out at dusk,
stayed out into the night. You would have gone out with
friends and family away from town and toward the cliffs.
Pufflings hatch in their nests on the cliffs, and when it is
time to leave they tumble out toward the water. For the
most part they bump along the cliff face or flutter in free-fall
until at last the surface of the water breaks and bobs and
holds them up. But sometimes they are blown back onto
land. The winds meeting the cliff are fierce. Often the pufflings try again, but sometimes they wander toward the
lights of town. Which is why the children of Heimaey
would break their own orbits, go out with cardboard boxes
to scoop them up and wait until daylight and then fling
them back off the cliff. Any grown-up on the island will
light up recalling how it was: like a month of Halloweens,
like a monthlong Easter egg hunt. But now the children
may go out only a night or two. The ocean water has been
warming and the food sources relocating, and there just
aren't that many pufflings to find there anymore.

IN ANY NUMBER OF WAYS, SIGURGEIR'S COLLECTION EVIDENCES
a kind of twinning, a kind of split, a doubling like a reflection in the water. Not only were there two sources of
birds, the lake and the shop, in time there were two taxidermists, too, to fuel his collecting: Steingrímur Þorsteinsson
in Dalvík, and Sigurður Guðmundsson, on the way, in Akureyri. When Sigurgeir chose the puffin and the northern

fulmar to accompany the grey heron home, he set a precedent, and his collection now is like a balanced scale: half
of it birds he brought in from the lake, and half of it birds
that could have come from anywhere but were nonetheless
birds he first laid eyes on in a taxidermist's shop.

I don't know why it should matter, birds from the lake or
birds from the shop, but it was somehow shocking when I
heard it. I had assumed there was something in the ritual,
that it was a collection not just of dead birds, but of dead
birds collected around this lake, a collection of all those phone
calls and all those farmers' freezers and all those pounds of
flesh. Indeed, I had at first assumed that Sigurgeir was himself a taxidermist, that the collection meant so much to his
family because it was his work, precocious and prodigious,
done there on the farm in a little shed. But what Sigurgeir
did was a different kind of making. It was not his hand that
mattered, but his eye. And surely every museum is a museum of selection, a museum of choices made, but here the
how of collecting seems not to matter. The source of a thing
does not matter. It is *the thing* that matters in its own right.
And that shouldn't shock me, surely it shouldn't, but when
was collecting ever just about things?

FOR A WHILE AFTER THE KRAFLA ERUPTION OF 1975, THE
government distributed wooden two-room sheds around
Mývatn and filled them with equipment to measure seis-
mographic activity. When the program ended eight years
later, the government took back the equipment but left the
sheds. I'd like to think that, knowing what they are, you
would recognize these shells when you see them, would
remember what they meant, but they are surprisingly non-
descript. They are essentially big wooden boxes with foot-

prints of 140 square feet and gently sloping roofs peaked symmetrically, right at the middle. I've never spotted another one anywhere in Iceland, but what could have happened to all those emptied husks? They say pintail ducks are "found widely in north-east Iceland but are nowhere common." Maybe the sheds are like that.

Or maybe everywhere there were people who had kept the machinery going, looked in on the readings, and reported back until the equipment was recalled. Maybe everywhere those people knew someone in the neighborhood who needed a room of their own—and here was a movable room. Or maybe that happened nowhere else. Maybe it was only the people who knew Sigurgeir and arranged for him to have it.

A picture of it survives: the day a massive truck delivered the shed to Sigurgeir's farm, tilting it off the bed toward the ground cleared and leveled to receive it. And there's Sigurgeir in the foreground, in a jean jacket, turned to the camera with an ecstatic smile.

The shed was surely more than one thing to Sigurgeir. It was a storage solution, of course. It was perhaps a sanctuary, fitted with shelves and lighting and an old bureau with eggs in every drawer. It was a space designated and defined, encapsulated, and it was—this must have mattered—a threshold and a door you could lock. The shed still stands there to this day. It's getting worn and torn as time goes by, but even now it keeps out the wind and the rain and the mice. It keeps safe fifty-nine birds, two foxes, and a mink. There's a hummingbird from Scottsdale, Arizona. Once an old lady from the next farm over gave Sigurgeir her collection of seashells—everything from this country, she said. The seashells, too, are still held in that shed.

IT USED TO BE THERE WAS A DIATOMIC FACTORY HERE pumping clay from the lake bottom, chugging and churning away, sucking up the calcium-laden corpses of ancient algae, all that industry to supply an ingredient to make toothpaste abrasive and cat litter absorbent and dynamite more stable. Sigurgeir worked there for twenty years, and for those twenty years things were much the same: working, driving, collecting. No girlfriend. No kids.

The lake is frozen two hundred days a year. Pumping the diatomaceous earth from its floor is possible only while the lake is thawed. Back on October 26, 1999, while Sigurgeir was working there, it was already late in the season. Indeed, the forecast was for frost.

They were hauling in the equipment when their efforts somehow broke a phone cable laid through the lake. So they found a phone connected to a different grid, a phone that still worked, and called the phone company offices, in Húsavík, who sent out a pair of men to make the repairs. When they arrived, Sigurgeir went back out with the two operators, one from Húsavík and one from Reykjavík, showed them where to look, and they fixed it. It was perfectly operational. And everything would have been fine, except they wanted to make sure it stayed fixed. They went out once more to weigh the cable down, sink it to the lake floor, where it would be safe and sound all winter. How much time could they spare? The forecast called for frost.

NO ONE SAW THE ACCIDENT.

AFTER A WHILE, WHEN IT HAD BEEN TOO LONG, A SEARCH party went out, walking and driving along the shore. I imagine the boots made sucking noises in the marsh. I imagine no one wanted to talk. The tires, rolling slowly along asphalt, must have made a static sound.

The rescue team included Sigurgeir's brother and brother-in-law. It was these two men who found him, here on the shore of this same peninsula. Not so very far from home, but gone. Gone. Sigurgeir was wearing a life jacket. The other two men from the boat drowned. Sigurgeir died from cold.

For days after, the phone at home on the farm was on the fritz. A blessing, perhaps, so the media didn't disturb the family. Anyway, they didn't need the phone. The family had walkie-talkies. They could call out if they wanted. But everything outside could wait.

I RENT A BIKE AT MY CAMPGROUND ON LAKE MÝVATN AND have my choice of eight helmets. Helmet in hand, I ask for a lock, which they keep on the shelf beneath the helmets, but the woman at the counter laughs. "This is Iceland," she says, and nothing happens.

Then she says, as if repeating the same three words but translated for my American ear: "Nothing gets stolen."

I look back at the rack of locks. Surely they exist for a reason.

"Really," she says, sending me out the door. "It's fine."

I'm a few miles out before I notice that there's not much of anything to lock a bike to in the first place—no trees, no bike racks, no poles unless they root a road sign to the ground. There is scrub and fog and midges and lava cooled into whorls like the grooves of massive fingerprints, and a sign where the road forks to the left to loop the lake and to the right to towns on the coast.

After the fork it's a few miles more to the museum and a long downhill and a retinue of birds chaperoning, calling at me, warning me not to cycle off the road and into their nests. As a group, they aggregate and dissolve again but keep a near-constant vigil for miles. Whimbrels, with their long, thin beaks and feet almost at a dangle, hover in my airspace and scream.

I have never given much thought to being a bird myself, but I begin to long for it, for some way to communicate with all these agitated fowl and assure them I have no intention of running off the road and smashing up their babies or their nesting grounds or their food source or whatever it is they are desperate to protect. But there is nothing for it but to cycle on.

SIGURGEIR WAS NOT THE FIRST SIBLING THE FAMILY LOST. In 1980 a different brother died, in a motorcycle accident in the fog. Some people say it was the fog. Some people say he was blinded by the sun. He was one year younger than Sigurgeir, and a boy who was always warm, since he was a kid, in T-shirts all summer in this country that has never recorded a temperature above 81 degrees Fahrenheit. He was just seventeen. It was only September, but he left for work from his mother's home complaining of feeling freezing cold. He never arrived at work.

The loss of the first son, it doesn't need saying, was tragic. The loss of a second son—and found by the last surviving brother—was too much to bear. And not just for the family. It galvanized the community. Something had to be done with all that grief. From all over, people wanted to help. There were more of them than you might think.

By then it had been custom, for at least fourteen years: If you had a friend visiting, you called Sigurgeir. Or maybe you didn't even call, you just dropped in to see his collection. A neighbor tells me, "A great number of houses have a bird or two or three," but this was a whole different order of magnitude. Sigurgeir had been interviewed on TV and in newspapers. The Icelanders and the tourists who knew about it came because Sigurgeir had so much more than a parlor collection, more than the centerpiece bird or the bookshelf birds you'd find in an average home.

As his sister describes it, there were "too many people to take into your living room." Groups as big as thirty would come over all at once. The shed was hard-pressed to accommodate. So at the point when Sigurgeir was gone but his birds were still there, his family figured there were three choices, maybe: make a museum, donate the collection to the state, or let it rot into the ground.

"Of course, we were foolish enough to select the most difficult and least sensible option. We started to build a real museum."

TO COLLECT STUFFED BIRDS IS NOT SUCH A RARE THING IN Iceland. The taxidermied skins, the birds after death, are a kind of species unto themselves, each adapted to its niche. There are the retail display birds, the restaurant decoration birds, a whole branch of various domestic aesthetic home decor birds on walls and shelves and coffee tables.

Indeed, there is a certain practice in Iceland of making a display of one's home window. Not everyone does it, and it's only ever one window of a home, a single stage, but there some combination of taxidermy or seashells or figurines or fake flowers in a little vase. Not a lot of things, not like storage, not the windowsill subbing as a bookshelf. No, just a few things, a spare kind of diorama: just a pair of black Converse shoes and a puffin posed on a rock.

And note in these cases, everything faces the street. The curtain is pulled so the passing viewer can see no farther into the life of this household than the windowsill tableau. The makers, and any evidence of their daily lives, are separated from their work. Maybe the windows act as landmarks. I think of these glimpses as a kind of charity, gifts to passersby. And maybe what's cast as centerpiece is a skull or a doll or a stuffed fox, but most likely it's a bird.

THERE WAS NO MODEL FOR THIS MUSEUM, THEY SAY. THEY say it was like inventing the wheel. It took four years just to get a permit to build so close to shore. The land is protected because, of course, the living birds are so important. The squabbling, preening, ruffled, feeding, courting, nesting, living birds. The balance of things is always delicate; a buffer of about 200 yards goes a long way.

After the permit was secured, it took another four years to build. "It's not easy to live around here and have an idea," a neighbor says with genuine distaste. "It's like chasing sheep." Then something in her face flickers and she smiles at me. "But then," she points out with all but a wink, "we are sheep farmers."

In hindsight the progression feels continuous, but there was a decade between Sigurgeir's death and the museum opening its doors. There's that much separation. It took that long to incubate. The collecting ended a long time before the museum came to bring visitors out of the farmhouse and out of the shed: before the museum came like an ether to fix the collection in its final form, in permanent exhibition.

One suspects the next generation, Sigurgeir's nieces and nephews, will take over when the time comes. They already have opinions and think it should expand. We'll see. Expansion is difficult in a place where everything needs to remain peaceful, unaltered, lest it disrupt the birds still to be seen on the water.

IT IS THE BEGINNING OF JULY. THE BIRDS ARRIVING AND courting and nesting peaked in May, and the bluster carried on into June, but now their displays are over and the drakes have flocked together to change their feathers. It is, of course, no more and no less than a group of male ducks gathered to molt the courting feathers and grow in a set better suited to migration. But it has the air of injury, of sulking, of licking their wounds—though one might as easily note their spirit of fraternity, clumped up as they are in grand old boys' clubs of chumminess. I like to imagine them almost monastic, retreating from the world as they witness their own helpless transformation.

While they idle, recover, and quite literally regroup, the drakes isolate themselves from the rest of duck life, the whole of duck society pulled away into two spheres like a cell dividing. Altogether, it will take a full month for the old feathers to fall and the new feathers to set. Which makes this also a month of mother ducks positively festooned with offspring, ornamented by their bobbing downy fluff and trailed by, echoed and encircled by, ducklings, everywhere.

AT SIX O'CLOCK THIS MORNING, ANY MORNING, STEFANÍA IS out feeding the cows with her sister and their mom. Her sister, the seventh child, is now the farmer here on the farm the seven siblings all grew up on. Their mother is eighty-five and dressed to work. This year there are 186 head of sheep, all presently on summer break up in the mountains. The cows, however, are always here: ten milking cows and nine beef cattle. Plus eleven chickens and one rooster, all the outbuildings to maintain, all the vehicles and machinery to keep going, and always a bed of rhubarb, sometimes struggling, sometimes thriving.

Stefanía runs the museum year-round. She comes in every day after the cows are fed. She mops the floors and keeps the books and plays host as visitors arrive. The three other sisters help when they can, the farmer and the banker and the kindergarten teacher. All in all, the museum is closed only five days a year. Stefanía is quiet and diligent and keeps her straight salt-and-pepper hair neatly bound at the nape of her neck. When I think of her, I think of her attentive gaze, her eyes alert and her hands busy with a broom handle or breaking bills to make change or serving a slice of spice cake from their grandmother's recipe. Silence seems to suit her, but if she's going to say something she takes care to get it right. To bridge my Icelandic and her English, she has charged the summer staff with answering my letters and sitting as interpreters when I visit.

Kristín is a woman with a kind of conspiratorial intensity and wide blue eyes, who spends her days off from the museum foraging medicinal herbs in the mountains. She translates her given name as literally "a Christian woman protected by Thor," and says of the juxtaposition, "There it is: the history of Iceland." Kristín lives a quarter turn around this lake, out by the first hotel, and has known Stefanía and Sigurgeir and their siblings since all of them were kids.

The museum sees ten thousand to twenty thousand visitors a year. Most come in the summer, but otherwise there is no pattern to it, no particular day of the week or time of day, unless it's that Icelanders are a little more likely to come on

Sundays. "Sunday you feel like you should do something," Kristín says. Otherwise, well, they come when they come. In waves. In trickles. In blots. Last year the museum's visitors represented some sixty-two nations. The birds themselves come from North America and Europe and Africa and kelp beds in the Atlantic Ocean. There are Germans who come here, not for the exotica of Icelandic birds they've never seen before, but to witness their own German birds here, in avian fancy dress, like they've never seen them at home.

THIS LAKE IS ONE OF THE FEW PLACES IN THE WORLD WHERE marimo grow, a kind of filamentous green algae also called lake goblins, lake rollers, or lake balls, for the way they pack into spherical forms, slowly rotating to catch the sunlight filtering down to the lake floor. *Marimo* translates literally from the Japanese as "a bouncy play ball plant that grows in the water." The Icelandic translates as "muck balls." They were first discovered in Austria not quite two hundred years ago, and have been found in only five countries in the world. They were noticed in Australia only as of 2014. Certainly no one knew they were here, in this very lake, a long way from Japan or Australia, until the rather recent date of 1978. They might be everywhere, if only we would look.

AS A CHILD, SIGURGEIR COLLECTED STAMPS, TOOK PICTURES, had a foreign coin collection, but for whatever reason, none of that took. He had these other forays into witnessing, into tokens of transport and circulation, but birds were his great calling. Maybe, had there been more time, there would have been another.

I'm told collecting is a thing that runs in families. It makes sense to me that families are cultures, that they propagate their values of what matters and what is normal and what we should do, but the idea is discussed like a genetic trait: a sensitivity, a capacity, a kind of special sight for what is significant and meaningful and should be held on to.

Stefanía is a collector of napkins, has been since she was a girl. All the napkin collectors I meet in Iceland are women, their collections begun as children, though no children do it now. It was a kind of custom for a time. You would go around after a baptism or a birthday party or a wedding and ask for a few spare napkins, and you'd trade with your friends for ones you didn't have. People who knew you would bring back napkins from a trip. In accumulation, these collections of paper ephemera track the holy days of a village or the evolution of air travel, outline a kind of ad hoc history of printing and interior design, observe an island nation getting rich enough to have disposable things. I've run into enough of these collections, been introduced to enough collectors, that I sometimes assume a napkin museum must be up and coming, is a kind of inevitability, must be on the horizon, a thing we can predict.

She shakes her head when I ask, says she couldn't possibly calculate how many she has stashed away, all those brimming boxes and plastic bags in her house on this farm. Maybe she will organize them later. Maybe when there's time. Maybe she will attend to her collection, when she isn't running this museum.

THEY SAY HE DREAMED OF A HOUSE FOR THE BIRDS. THEY SAY that he said he didn't mind where. A "proper house," he said, a house for display. The bird on the museum logo is a Barrow's goldeneye. It has a dot pupil in the center of its circular eye in the middle of its bulbous bonce. These birds are not possessive of their offspring, sometimes laying eggs in other nests. Indeed, the ducklings of several different broods often come together under the care of one female, one caretaker for all those birds.

The goldeneye is a medium-sized diving duck, but more to its essence, it is a duck that likes to have a roof, a shelter. In the Rocky Mountains it puts its eggs in a tree. In Iceland, where there is still a lively debate as to whether the island ever had trees or only ever scrub, the goldeneye puts its eggs in lava caves and the rock walls of houses, though it will nest on the ground if it has to. Its only breeding ground that can be said to be in Europe is in this northern region of Iceland, hosting some two thousand pairs a year. Otherwise it's a North American bird, though it bears noting that the species was first described from a population found here, and wherever it has gone since, it is from this outpost in Iceland that the goldeneye takes its origin story, its species name, *islandica*.

Yet in Iceland it is not an *islandica*. In Iceland, it is a *húsönd*, a house duck. And I think about how beautiful that is, how appropriate, how lovely that the house duck represents Sigurgeir's Bird Museum, this home for the collection, this house they say he dreamed of. That is the story I tell myself, the lovely thing I think until I learn that the final addition, the very last birds to come into Sigurgeir's collection, were none other than a pair of goldeneyes, one male and one female.

I don't have the nerve to ask if maybe that's why the family picked that bird as the icon, if the bird meant something more to the people who knew. If what they see in all its circles is last and final and end. And I don't wonder if Sigurgeir was waiting on them, the pair of goldeneyes, if he had any special plans or was eager to bring them home or had scheduled the trip to collect them from the taxidermist's shop. Because my heart breaks every time I remember that he didn't.

It was his youngest sister, the farmer, who went to the shop in Dalvík, to pick up the goldeneyes when they were ready, after he was gone.

SIGURGEIR'S BIRD MUSEUM IS FITTED WITH TWO TELESCOPES. It is stocked with postcards and drink ware and maps and books and DVDs and carved birds and ice cream bars and a video monitor with all kinds of information on the birds outside. From the windows in the museum's entryway you can see the lake and the sky and the plants and the birds. You can see the farm. There's nothing to tell you that you wouldn't even be in this museum entryway, wouldn't have the museum or these windows to look out in the first place, if it hadn't been for everything that happened before you, happened in those buildings and in this lake and on these shores. The brochure claims, "Sigurgeir's Bird Museum is considered the largest private bird collection that is known in Iceland." One only wonders about collections yet unknown.

The lake is home to forty-five regular breeding bird species, and Iceland as a whole sees seventy-seven. But of course more species than that have found these shores. The list of just exactly which species are currently regulars is to some degree a judgment call and, in any case, in flux, but the museum finished its accounting a long time ago. Whatever happens outside its walls, the museum is home to a constant two hundred birds—Sigurgeir's birds—and ninety-nine species of egg.

The gyrfalcon and the snowy owl in the museum are fifty years old, older than the laws that now protect them, the present of an old man who had kept them in his living room. You couldn't collect them now, but because these specimens found their way to Sigurgeir, the museum collection is all but complete. Indeed, for the time being, it boasts every modern Icelandic species save one.

The holdout is þórshani, a small wading bird, a kind of sandpiper that inexplicably spends nearly the entire year out at sea. We say it is a wading bird, but eleven months out of the year it's set up in beds of seaweed or picking parasites off the backs of whales. It's known in Icelandic as Thor's rooster but more widely as the red phalarope. Its plumage is so different in these arctic places where it breeds that most of Europe knows it the rest of the year by a different costume, and accordingly refers to it, the very same bird, as the *gray* phalarope. Its song, I cannot resist telling you, is described as a "sharp metallic kreeep."

They are noted for the females, which are bigger and brighter than the males, rust-colored from the neck down with pale blue legs. These are ladies who court and call and pursue the males, then lay a clutch and leave those two or three or four eggs to be incubated by the males while they fly on. It's a striking division of labor, how one can lay eggs, while the other takes over from there. I think about the difference between founders and those who maintain, the spark it takes to begin and the will to soldier on. It can be hard in other circumstances to disentangle, but here the act of creation is so clearly distinguished from the ensuing but entirely separate act of caretaking. I'm not saying it's any better than any other way of doing things, but it seems worth noting how each has its role and each gets its due, this promise of parity, or at least that something might be split in half and survive.

It's Kristín who tells me about the phalaropes, saying they are one of the last birds to arrive in the spring. It used to be they would come all at once, in one flock that would blot out the sun. "There was a tradition of leaving all you were doing and welcoming them."

Imagine it: that moment when you noticed. It must have been a thing you sensed, a thing that struck you, a thing that made you stand still. What a holy moment, that beat before you pricked your ears to confirm or lifted your eyes to check that it was happening, this annual occasion you could count on but couldn't control, happening exactly now, this instant, today. Perhaps Sigurgeir's grandmother knew these days without having to be told.

There are plenty who remember, but there's no such tradition anymore—Kristín says there hasn't been since the Gulf War, when drying the wetlands was a military tactic. I can't confirm the cause, but the phalaropes were decimated, their numbers dropping 90 percent. This happened in living memory. They say the phalaropes are recovering now. But they no longer blot out the sun.

IF YOU ARE WONDERING WHAT BIRDS ARE ON THE WATER, you don't even have to ask. The museum has a whiteboard on display, detailing all the birds sighted on the lake as of yesterday. The names are wiped away each morning and the marker uncapped and the record renewed. Yesterday there were twenty-one species seen, and today Stefanía has written them out in blue strokes on the list, on this slate where there are only ever two points of reference: what happened yesterday and how it is known today.

Today the museum collection sits, as it has since it opened, under one roof. It is a dark room, but the light is good. It is not exactly quiet; it is something more like still. *Solemn* is perhaps the word. Not grave, but perhaps a little like holding your breath. It is a room that sets you, at your leisure, on a circular path that arrives at a place where you can no longer continue. There are no signs to say so, no rise in the floor to warn you, no railings to keep you from taking the one long step that would carry you over.

It is a room interrupted. Seen from above, the exhibition room is a regular polygon fitted with a circular pond in the center. That center-point pond is like the head of a keyhole, from which issues a wedge of water that runs to the wall. The channel is sunk into the ground, the room impossible to circumnavigate without somehow fording this riparian feature, the spring flowing across the room and out of it, under a pair of doors that no one opens.

There is a roof with twelve radiating beams, and cases snug along the perimeter walls. A first set of cases radiate from the center like spokes, and the angles they make are bisected by yet another set of cases, a second corona. The path through is not entirely set, but more or less one counterclockwise rotation. One arrives at the water cut through the floor and doubles back, retracing the same path, rewinding the clock.

THE FIRST BIRD I LEARNED TO CALL BY NAME IN ICELANDIC was the *kría*, the arctic tern. This was by necessity, a bird I needed a name for, its name so easy to remember, almost onomatopoeic, for the screech it issued while hurtling in a dive bomb toward my head. I was in the northern coastal city of Húsavík, and met the *kría* anytime I tried to run the

road past the edge of town. I studied them on Grímsey island, the only bit of Iceland that crosses the arctic circle, an
island of one hundred people, each of them outnumbered
by birds one thousand to one. The *kría* are crisply cut, all
clean edges and sharp sounds. They have black caps and
white breasts and tails forked like serpents' tongues. They
do not nest so much as lay their eggs in a depression in the
ground, in some smattering of scrub, and defend their precious clutch of two plus or minus one, through a systematic
campaign of alarm calls and air attacks.

It is terrifying. Not only the cry itself, which is bad, but the
Doppler shift of a thing accelerating toward you, cutting a
razor-straight path to pierce your crown with its needle-nosed
orange beak. The instinct is startling, how swiftly one cringes
and ducks. I was told to walk holding a stick or a folded umbrella up in the air, because they aim for the highest point of
their enemy. I've heard photographers love to point their long
lenses skyward and shoot. I was told the terns never actually

hurt anyone, but I've seen them make contact with those nips. I've heard yelps. I've seen them take hair.

I learned that wearing a brimmed hat helps immeasurably, like blinders on a horse, that catching the plummet out of the corner of my eye was the worst of it, and if I could disconnect the sound and the motion, the scream and its source, I hardly minded one alone. If you could cleave them, they became something else.

I ENTER THE MUSEUM COLLECTION THROUGH A SET OF BLUE double doors that frame a case of seabirds. The entry doors are the mirror image of the doors just adjacent, under which the water drains out of the room. Most birds in the cases are noted with their Icelandic name and five translations. There is a calendar marked with their months in Iceland, and both a summer and a winter map of their territory. So many Icelandic birds aren't always in Iceland, aren't even mostly in Iceland. The *kría*, for instance, have to make it to Antarctica before they come back again the next year to lay their eggs, and they aren't even known to take a direct route to the other side of the world.

The button above each square blue label, when pushed, illuminates a tiny blue light at the base of the bird it references. I press the button for the great cormorant, with its green eyes. I light up a whimbrel, like the ones that herd me along the road on my bike, and then a king eider and a baby whooper swan.

I learn that I like the velvet scoter, even the black scoter, both of them types of black ducks with bills the very satisfying color of blood oranges. I enjoy the snowy bouffant of the long-tailed duck, a bird like a Sunday hat. I like the whimbrel and the glossy ibis for the curve of their bills, something I did not notice about any of the whimbrels that had escorted me here, a thing I had not even considered as they opened those curved bills and rent the air.

Sigurgeir's Bird Museum doesn't draw much attention to Sigurgeir. His name is there, of course. But it would be easy enough to visit the museum, stay long enough to have a waffle and a coffee served by his sister, and never think of the man directly. It would be easy enough not to notice that this is a memorial museum. Or maybe it registers, the palpable sense of something honored—indeed, beautifully so—but without ever being able to place its source. It feels so essential to me, the way this place and its story are bound up inextricably with each other, and yet it isn't said or doesn't need to be. It isn't intended to be a museum about grief or separation or chance events. Surely the birds are enough.

There are more specimens back at the farmhouse or still out in the old shed. Those are the repeat species, the exclusively foreign fowl, the birds and the beasts that for one reason or another didn't fit in the museum. The collared dove and the hooded crow are there, the kingfisher and bee-eater, the bullfinch and the turtledove, black grouse and golden oriole.

I consider, briefly, why one collects not just birds but also eggs. The one seems to me hardly to do with the other. They are connected, of course, not just obviously but also originally, ultimately—and yet when I think about a bird, I do not begin to consider its beginning. Even the collection keeps them separate. Sure, a bird may be shown *en scène* with a nest and some eggs and faux guano rained on them for good measure—but the eggs qua eggs are like spare lightbulbs, clean as geometry, three cases just of eggs, displayed without nest or bird or guano or anything. These eggs do not even touch each other. They are spaced at regular intervals across shallow shelves, with shelf stacked over shelf like rungs on a ladder.

Maybe if I knew something of shells breaking—not under my hand in the kitchen, but without warning—with birds in them, I might then make the connection. Mostly when I have thought about eggs, if I have thought about them at all, it has been as symbols, as beginnings. Only here does it occur to me that they are as easily read in reverse, as finality, as the punctuation to some other process, some other series of events. I stand in this room, stand still, facing a case with eggs enough to fill my field of vision. I will leave soon, bike the rest of the way around the lake, and stop for dinner, saddle sore. But they will remain here, like this, indefinitely. I watch the eggs under glass and their perfect reflection. If I stand just so, their reflection inside the glass doubles and redoubles, the hollow shells reproduced, a line not quite straight but predictable, lifting up and back, to infinity.

The Museum of Icelandic Polar Bears

*T*he polar bear. No one has given it a nickname, but it is built into the house.

Or, *It landed here starving.*

Or, *This is an exhibition on the dream of flight, and here in the corner, our polar bear. You see he did the feet wrong. They should be pointed in, not straight ahead.*

No polar bear is Icelandic, unless for those few hours between when they manage to swim ashore, emaciated, and are shot. But from that moment on, they are here forever. There may be nothing more Icelandic than a taxidermied polar bear. They dot the country, museum by museum, one per town, requisite in the local history museum, the local collection of natural history. It does not matter that they are nothing local to begin with, or that the bear you see almost never landed here.

And yet, from its distribution, you might think it was the national animal—totemic, talismanic, necessary. And maybe it should be, this creature washed here from another country, this creature of arctic waters and fish, this creature animated by and dying of hunger.

I see enough that I begin to think of it all as one unnamed museum, borderless, the museum of Icelandic polar bears. It has scores and scores of specimens. All its doors are open. It will be so easy for you to see one, and when you

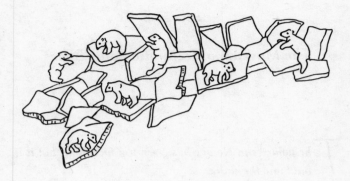

see one, you start to see them all. You will only ever see them in this everywhere museum. Indeed, I suspect, you cannot see one anywhere else.

MADE OF

DRIFTWOOD

FULL OF

WORMHOLES

Skógar Museum

(Skógasafn)

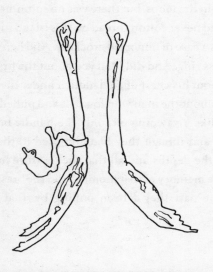

Here is a church made from sixteen churches. Here is its shipwreck beam. Here is a hay saddle with a whalebone peg, and here is a Danish two-kronur coin. There are audio recordings from 1904. There are shackles everywhere. There's a millstone imported from Norway, but the heron legs, cut from living birds in longing and magical thinking that it would make the sailors return home safely, those are locally sourced. And notice how singular objects don't need initials carved in their sides—a unique enough thing needs no further distinction—but the stuff of plenty is marked up in ownership, personalized in that way, so that at the end of haying season, everyone can take back what is theirs.

This is a museum without sequence. Even the guides say you can start anywhere. It all links, they say. And maybe it doesn't matter in what order you learn that driftwood, too, was marked to claim it on the beach, that putrefied skate is a delicacy the day before Christmas Eve, that there was no salt to preserve the catch until the nineteenth century, just all that cod all those years dried in the Arctic winds.

I might as well tell you now that knitting came from the Germans, in the 1600s, but there was no spinning wheel until 1740, and never cotton thread on this island full of sheep. And here's a case of imported crockery. And here's a church door's brass ring. And did I tell you about the first settler of Skógar, about his chest of gold hidden under the Skógafoss waterfall, about the men who found it and pulled it up from a crevice like a yawning pit, only the handle broke under the strain and though they had glimpsed it, the chest fell back into the depths and all that the treasure hunters had left was the memory of that moment and the brass ring of its handle, the part they'd been pulling by, that torn-away

souvenir, and did I tell you how that ring from the chest became the ring of this church door?

ICELAND'S BIGGEST MUSEUM OUTSIDE REYKJAVÍK FITS IN A
town of twenty-one people. Not even a town, but a hamlet,
a *dreifbýli*: a "someplace" shy even of the fifty persons it
takes to make a town in Iceland. You could miss it. You
could miss both the someplace and the museum in it when
you turn off the southern stretch of ring road for Skógar;
though, if you know what you're looking for, you can see
it from the exit. The hamlet is off to the right side of the
exit, and a churning, pounding, curtains-of-mist waterfall
is off to the left. In the fields below the waterfall, a carpet of
ponchos and pop-up tents bloom as bright as wildflowers.
Above them, high above the rustling of tarps, hundreds of
campers and hikers and day-trippers steadily ascend the
switchbacks and stairs, finally come even with that place,
that definable edge, where a river runs out of bed and becomes something else.

The Skógar Museum comprises fifteen thousand objects, plus a village's worth of historic structures and lately
a new transportation collection just adjacent. The gravel
parking lot is dotted with museum pieces parked among
the vehicles that come and go: the four-wheel-drives and
economical little rental cars and idling white tour buses,
which are somehow both massive and sleek. The original
collector still lives next door, within shouting distance of
his life's work. He was ninety-five years old when we met
and working on his twenty-fourth book—it's about milk—
and just recently retired as the museum's curator, though
I've heard he wasn't ready, that he thought it happened all

too soon. He keeps a lovely garden. I'm told he has beautiful handwriting, still. And it's all here, the collection and the curator and the museum and the parking lot and the tour buses and maybe the garden, too, all because this someone in this someplace, a long time ago, was given a quest.

Þórður Tómasson was fourteen when it happened. There was an old woman living in the house with them. You could say she cast a spell. That's what the guide says. She cast a spell when she pressed into his hand an object flat and brass. She told Þórður, "Never give this away." She told him it mattered.

We don't know why she picked him, if he was sweet or pliant or careful or cunning. If she saw something special in him, or if she had no other heir. We don't know if this was a gift to him, or if his taking care of it was more of a favor to her. We don't know what she thought would happen next, but I assume there was a light in her eyes. I assume he had no idea what was coming, that this moment would still matter to him in any way when he was ninety-five. But we know this was the beginning. We mark this as the first thing. And we know that thereafter, Þórður began to keep a great many things.

IN THE YEAR 1000, OR MAYBE THE YEAR BEFORE, ICELAND became a Christian nation. Or at least, with a single official decision, it declared itself a less openly pagan state. It happened overnight, as they like to say, and without a drop of blood. When not enough grain could be grown to make communion wafers, the pope himself made dispensation that Icelanders might make the body of Christ from dried fish.

In 1550 Iceland converted again, to Protestantism, and this time there was so much to be erased. Priests and bishops were killed; the art and the altars of churches were burned, destroyed, stamped out of memory—tabula rasa. It's as if we could not adopt a new religion then without destroying an old one. They say crosses were generally spared, but otherwise the kinds of things that usually survive over time, those things that are rare or expensive, that get handed down, that are granted that strange protection of occasional use, were exactly the kinds of precious, symbolic objects that were purged. There's a lot missing from those centuries; it's hard to say how much. But it spans half the history of Iceland, and we do not get it back.

THE SOUTHERN COAST OF ICELAND RUNS A GOOD THREE hundred miles without a harbor. It's just too shallow, with too much shifting sand. The new ferry terminal at Landeyjahöfn is forever dredging anew the same short path, that the new ferry may again return to shore. Whereas places like Keflavík and Reykjavík and Grindavík and Húsavík and Hólmavík and Dalvík are named for their bays—bays of the valley or of the home or of the steam venting from the earth thick as smoke—the southern village of Vík has no prefix, needs no distinguishing specification; it is not a thing of plenty, would never be confused with a neighboring bay, because there are none.

It's a form of isolation. If there is no safe harbor, there is no trade, no commerce, no visitors save those who walk or ride, those precious few travelers who traverse the low flat stretches, leaning into a wind that is so stop-you-still fierce because it is so baldly unencumbered. That traffic, historically, was not nothing. There were farms. There were monasteries. But this is a geography that slows a certain kind of movement, a certain kind of growth. The south is a part of the country that does not talk about east and west but of east and *out*—unless one is talking about going to Reykjavík, that smoky bay, which somehow, not geographically but in the language, is always a matter of going *south*. And all the while, all those glacial rivers run to the sea, keep the land of the south inaccessible, keep washing away its bridges, even now.

Southern Iceland has been continuously inhabited for about as long as there have been Icelanders. The region was the landing shore of the Norse settlers and before them the Gaelic monks, who carved their style of crosses into cave walls. That means there have been inhabitants since the year 874, or the year 800, or possibly much earlier—but all that time there was no town to speak of, until a hundred years ago, when the early bridges were built.

That's how it was around 1920, when a new national law required, for the very first time, that every county build a school. Mind you, Iceland had instituted mandatory literacy in the sixteenth century, and since the seventeenth century, formal education had been a matter of traveling tutors coming to live at your farm one month a year. This education was a guaranteed right of every Icelander. And if you were extra lucky, maybe you'd also be sent over to the bishop's wife to learn to play the organ.

The museum at Skógar exists because two adjacent counties found themselves each with populations too slim to justify building schools for their children. They didn't have enough people and they didn't have enough resources. Skógar was near the border of these two places, and in 1940—a few years after a boy of that southern coast was made beholden to a bit of brass—a farmer donated a parcel of Skógar land so that there might be one school shared between them. The museum in Skógar exists because there was going to be a school. Or perhaps, more to the heart of it, it exists because there was already a reverend.

JÓN GUÐJÓNSSON WANTED TO BE AN ARCHITECT. BUT HE would have had to leave Iceland to study—go to Denmark or Germany—and so, looking for something secure, something that could be done without leaving the country, something with a short course of study to land a job, he ended up a man of God. The reverend Jón, as he was known, was a tall man, wore enormous shoes. He and his wife had ten children. I'm told he must have been a charming man to the ladies in his youth. They say he was remarkable, hardworking, very industrious, extremely nice, and not especially religious.

He's known best nowadays for founding the folk museum in Akranes, where he wrote all the tags, did all the fund-raising, and kept precise records of everything. When the cement factory opened, he waited to get the first bag. When a factory for nylon stockings was up and running, he got the first pairs. They say he was never paid for his work.

They say he would phone you late at night. They say after you poured him a drink in your parlor, he'd walk home a young man. But there's one story I've heard, and it's how I always imagine him: Jón alone in the Akranes folk museum, totally absorbed, working on a diorama with exacting little strokes. Who knows how long the phone rings before he hears it? Phone to his ear, brush, I assume, still in hand, he hears the voices of his congregants, all assembled at church at the appointed time, reminding him that perhaps he might join them and lead the Sunday service.

There is much to say about the reverend Jón, about his

museum in Akranes, the one where he grew old, about the cluster of boats he managed to acquire for the museum but struggled vainly to maintain, about what it means to always start with a little money and then have none. But beneath all that there's Skógar: the story of Jón's first museum, the story of the second museum in Iceland.

The reverend Jón arrives at the southern parish in 1934; by 1946 he'll be gone. Had he been an itinerant preacher, a Jónny Appleseed of collections, there might have been museums everywhere, dotting the countryside, but there will only ever be the two by his hand. He stays in that southern parish just over a decade, long enough to initiate a collecting committee of three individuals, including a young Þórður Tómasson.

The reverend Jón has already quit the parish when the group of three collectors officially donate their findings and establish the museum collection in the bottom of the Skógar school in 1949. He is gone for the winter storage, the summer exhibits. He is not there in 1959, when Þórður is finally engaged with the museum in a formal capacity, as its first and until recently only curator. Indeed, the reverend Jón is gone for almost all of it.

And yet—and this bears noting—his time in the southern parish, however brief, was enough. The reverend Jón is outlived by two museums because, at least on that one day long ago, it was enough for a parish priest to say at a borderland farm: If we are going to build a school, we should build in it a museum.

THERE ARE SO MANY FLAVORS OF LOSS. THERE IS DEPRIVATION and disappointment. There is sacrifice and grief. There is trifling. There is needless. There is missing and forgotten. There is, though sometimes it is hard to imagine, necessary. There is, though we hardly need reminding, catastrophic.

Iceland trades in all of them, every gradation of loss and lack and disappearance. It is a population that hovered near fifty thousand for centuries and centuries, that didn't hit six digits until 1926, but that every so often is astonishingly diminished. The guide at the museum says of Iceland, "That is the incredible story: how anyone survived at all."

Historically, the threats were legion. Maybe it's an epidemic or a famine or an eruption. The black plague killed a third of the island in 1402. Smallpox was just as deadly in 1707. Between 1751 and 1758, a famine claimed six thousand lives.

The Laki eruption alone, the one in 1783, killed 20 percent of Icelanders and 80 percent of their livestock. It altered the sky. In modern times that eruption would keep planes grounded for three years. It affected farmers as far away as Japan, and the resulting crop failures in Europe can credibly be thought to have sparked the French Revolution. The famine that followed the floods and the fumes and the ash killed another quarter of the Icelandic population. The toll was so devastating that Denmark, not necessarily known for its generosity to its colonies, offered to evacuate the whole island. The Danish authorities had, and not without reason, come to the conclusion that Iceland was uninhabitable.

But the Icelanders stayed. They stayed another century, and then it was the mass emigrations of the nineteenth century that carried many of them away, all those Icelanders in all those ships, setting sail for promises in Brazil and Manitoba and Utah.

*

WHEN THE REVEREND JÓN SAID, "WE SHOULD, YOU KNOW, build a museum as long as we're building a school," there was at that time exactly one museum in the whole of Iceland. There had only ever been exactly that one museum, and it had been the only museum in Iceland for eighty years.

You could argue that the notion to keep collections is old beyond record, old as ages, old as the ability to stash or carry, old like species are old. But museums, you could argue, are a more recent development. There's certainly an era, a couple of centuries back, when it became a fashion for the nation-states of Europe to express their nation building, consolidate their national identities, through the founding and development of national museums. Museums were a kind of national project, a point of national pride. And Iceland, back then, was the kind of Danish colony that wanted to become a nation.

If you are going to make a bid for independence, one thing to do is make a claim for who you are. It's not that you're disrupting the status quo by suddenly becoming independent; you're just asserting a sovereignty that was essentially always there—inherently, naturally, obviously there—except for a while you were too busy to mention it. And if you are indeed such an independent people, obviously you have a distinct history and culture all your own—and just look! Here in this museum. You have the stuff to prove it!

Before Iceland had independence (in 1944), before it had sovereignty (in 1918), before it had home rule (first in 1874 and expanded in 1904), it had a museum. The National Museum of Iceland, Þjóðminjasafn Íslands, was established in 1863. Note that contents to fill it had to be recalled from the collections of Denmark's national museum, with an especially significant transfer in 1930. Note that that's how this works.

The Icelandic collection shifted around Reykjavík for a few decades, then settled in the attic of the national library for a good forty years. That's where it was when the Kingdom of Iceland became the Republic of Iceland, an independent nation, back in 1944. Its very first act of parliament: to build a house for the national museum. The National Museum of Iceland was a collection in the attic of a library, had been for some time, when the Reverend Jón proposed a museum in the basement of a school that did not yet exist.

THEY SAY THE THING THAT CHANGED ICELAND WAS THE rubber boot. They say that for a thousand years there was nothing for it, the damp and the wet, shoes cut like slippers instead of boots, a kind of minimum—of material, of investment, of separation from the ground—and so ephemeral anyway, the wrap of fishskin or sealskin or sheepskin cupping the sole soon scored and sliced to tatters, inevitably, from walking the volcanic earth.

But eventually there was an inescapable war, and the British landed, and the Americans soon enough, and nothing ever keeps confined to a military encampment. They say the rubber boot was a revelation. They say that the Icelanders had spent a thousand years with wet feet, and now even a fisherman could come home with dry toes. They say it was a shock. The dryness was too foreign, too unsettling, too drastic to be borne. So radical was the change, they say some people sometimes poured a little water into their rubber boots, an intervention, to make them feel right again.

From the Norsemen to the Second World War, Iceland

lived in the middle ages. That's how the Icelanders say it. All that time before, all those Icelanders in houses with no tables or chairs, with two or three people in a bed and those beds too short to lie down in. So much of that time working in the dark, in those main rooms named for the old saunas, *baðstofa*, even though the island had long since been denuded of the wood to burn to heat a sauna, and long since plunged into a little ice age that left the island colder even than during the sauna years.

Indeed, by one kind of accounting, there had never been much to begin with, not the stuff of civilization, not on this island where the wood had long ago been burned, where everything was built from driftwood or shipwreck or turf cut from the ground, where there was essentially no usable metal or workable clay to be dug from the ground, and anyway no heat source hot enough to work them. Children's toys were bones and shells. There was no national dance and not much music, and the national costume was first dreamed up not by custom but by a designer, and even that only a hundred years ago. We know the date the first well-meaning priest planted the first potato in Icelandic soil to keep people from starving, but there was never a date for it sprouting.

These days there are greenhouses, now that the geothermic heat is better harnessed, and they do all right with cucumbers and tomatoes and such viny veg. But essentially, on this island, for a thousand years, no resource was kept at home when it could be sold abroad—the salt fish, the whale oil, the herring, and with no guarantee what could be fished next year.

This is a country where the first bridges didn't come until 1920. This is a land of people so used to all things pickled, salted, and dried that there are still Icelanders alive today who believe fresh food makes you sick, who ask if you've been eating fresh food if you look a little thin or pale or ill, who limit themselves to a few canned strawberries for Christmas.

But once the change happened, it happened so fast—in three decades, maybe. Modernization compressed to unfold in a generation. It wasn't just the rubber boot, of course. It was World War II and independence from Danish rule and the influence of American occupation. It was the first transatlantic cable and motorized fishing boats and passenger air travel. It was, for a time, the herring swimming close and enough fortunes made before those silver schools rerouted themselves elsewhere. Arguably the whole postwar world was changing quickly, but Iceland started from such a deficit, was among the poorest nations in Europe for so long—when it wasn't winning the title outright—that even to catch up in the twentieth century, to shake off foreign rule for the first time, to have some money, was to leapfrog a whole way of life.

THEY SAY IT'S 1950 WHEN THE OLD SOCIETY ENDS. THE PEOPLE leave turf houses for stone. The farms get machines. You couldn't miss it. A nation decamping from a way of life. A whole society leveling up. The first supermarkets opened in 1955, the first apartment blocks were constructed in the 1960s, the first Icelandic television station went on the air in 1966. They say the first things to be burned were the bed boards, those planks of wood, often carved, that converted the bed from a seating area during the day to a place to sleep at night, the bed board like a rail or a gate to keep dreamers from falling out of a narrow bed and onto the narrow dirt floor.

There is a narrative of obsolescence in all this, of modernization as a sudden stripping away of everything that was no longer relevant, a kind of nationwide three-decades-long, well-overdue, good-for-the-soul spring cleaning.

But there is also a narrative of shame, of an after that had no use for before. This is the story of how a thousand years of toil and want and misery sounded as it rang out from the old things, a constant memory of less than and not enough, and how given the chance to forget, the Icelanders wasted no time, cleaved these haunting thoughts and the things they attached to and endeavored to start afresh. This, at long last, was a loss they could control.

I ALWAYS IMAGINE THE FIRST PHASE OF THIS TRANSITION like a flood. I imagine such a rush to let go, be done, move on, that anyone looking could have seen it happening. That it changed the landscape. And how easy it must have been to go with that flow, to share in the shedding, to pour out the old. But if this was a nation looking firmly ahead, all future tense and aspiration, there were pockets of resistance. Þórður Tómasson had already started collecting. He had already been told that it mattered.

In those days of outpouring and momentum, Þórður was like a boulder in the current. Everything washed past him. In the face of so much cultural and material transformation, he had only to dissent, to stay the course, to keep collecting, to embrace what wasn't wanted and gather it up, capture some fraction of that outflow of obsolescence and divert it from the junkyards, the bonfires, until there was a reservoir of the rejected set aside, a still pond of memory that otherwise could have been erased.

What was it like to be a young man who collected things then? Was this a form of rebellion in an age of turnover, an era when everything that had made up life for a thousand years was traded in, shrugged off, retired and not replaced? The turf houses, always threatening to dissolve, to cave in, to sink under their own weight and rejoin the ground they were cut from, were finally left to follow through on their imperative. A thousand years of constant repairs and then nothing. Surely collecting meant one thing to Þórður in his youth and something different in middle age and something else now. Surely it is almost painfully complicated. And yet as a mission, as a foundational quest, it is so unflinchingly simple.

Remember, you're asking just for what can be parted with. Indeed, in all likelihood, you are asking only to be the one to take away what has already been set aside or put out or left neglected in the barn. The donation need not be a sacrifice. And *donation* is the word. Among the fifteen thousand objects in the collection, maybe five or ten were purchased—the Icelandic side saddle on auction in Copenhagen, for instance—but everything else was gathered and given. Over decades you take away all those things, one by one and lot by lot. But in their place you leave your neighbors with a story.

No one talks about the thing you took away—who wanted it anyway? They talk about the curious fellow who came looking. And as word spreads, about you, about your peculiar enthusiasm, it is not just a solitary quest of you seeking out the things but also, increasingly, the stewards of those things now seeking out you. There comes a tipping point. Now it's not just the things that were going to be thrown out that come your way, but the sentimental things, too, the things people keep until they can find them a good home.

There is a saying in Iceland: If you plant a tree, you'll get more trees in the same place. And here is the genius of Þórður's collecting: It began to perpetuate itself. Yes, there was a wave of asking, of going from farm to farm, of criss-crossing the south, moving farther and farther from home, like a pendulum somehow picking up speed. There were the days, there were always days, when Þórður went out just to buy fish and came back with rare books. But go out enough and it invites a second kind of wave, of others coming to you.

Once you have a reputation, maybe it takes the edge off. Maybe you know things are working their way to you. Maybe you feel you can get in front of it. Maybe you don't mind waiting, say, for those ice skates set with bone as blade, in use until 1972 but eventually here, hung by their laces on the museum wall, the bone cutting nothing but air.

THE STUFF IN THIS MUSEUM IS POOR PEOPLE'S STUFF. THAT'S what the guide says. As in dung forks and turf knives and plows. Or else we're talking about the wooden shovel, the washing cudgel, the waffle iron, the candle mold. Or maybe it's the flat irons, the yardsticks, the whale stomach, the line float—the mass of it all too much to take in, eyes a-stutter, attention skip-skimming across such a strata of survival: a grindstone, a potstone, a scale from a shop. Seventy percent of the wooden things are made from driftwood, and so much of it all dates back at least to the nineteenth century, to a time when one in seven people in Iceland hosted a tape-worm in their gut.

Never mind all the stuff that isn't here, the things never made or never replaced for lack of resources, the things used and reused and repaired and repurposed and chipped and cracked and tattered and frayed and splintered and bruised and torn and scuffed and scrubbed and shattered and worn until gone. These are just the things we have that weren't consumed or obliterated, a subset of the things we could possibly have, a subset of the things there were.

Where there are museum records of these items, the records are all provenance. Even if you wanted to, there's no field to note the material substance of a thing. The museum log starts from the very first item collected, but in all that time from then to now it has never been the what of the thing that matters, compared to the import of the who and the where: who gave it, who used it, where it's from. It's always been the story that mattered most, the connections inferred, the object not as a thing of inherent properties but as a touchstone to who we are and where we come from. In a certain light, these records aren't even a matter of provenance so much as kind of alternative genealogy.

Icelanders, especially on Sundays, and especially if there's a family connection to the region, are in here asking for the pieces donated by their kin. The mitten lifeline. The suits drenched in cod-liver oil once a year. "I was in that rowboat," they say. "I sat on that stool when my grandmother washed the sheets." And the museum is strikingly well suited to answer.

Not that you open the records. Not that they need to be consulted. Not until recently. Because the museum was formally founded in 1949 and formally housed in 1954, and Þórður Tómasson was formally hired as its first curator in 1959 and how could the records he kept compare to the man himself, when at all times he keeps in his mind the lineage of half the country?

Maybe he studied your face, and told you before you

spoke even a word who your people were. Maybe you gave him your name and straightaway he showed you to the textile your grandmother gave him. Maybe he talked with you for a while and then disappeared, came back with the phone in his hand and the announcement, "It's for you." Because he had put the pieces together and identified a distant cousin you didn't know you had, just two fjords over, and called them up and here they are, inviting you over for coffee, when you put the phone to your ear.

For half a century Þórður personally guided everyone who came in. The log doesn't record where any given thing is in the museum, partly because Þórður was prone to reconfiguring and never seemed satisfied that the story was settled or the collection complete, but mostly because as long as he was there, why would it? He knew. He had taken such care to know everything he could about the things he had. You'd arrive at the museum and he'd take an instrument off the wall and play it. His drop spindle demonstration was all down to muscle memory, the expert movement of the spindle off his thigh practiced into instinct.

But when people talk about the museum, they don't talk about his expertise or his doggedness or even the book he compiled on Icelandic words for weather, a collection of language no single Icelander had ever known in its entirety before because the words, as indeed the weather itself, were so regionally specific. What people talk about, what they remember, are these moments when the museum was made intimately, unarguably their own.

Nothing makes me want to be an Icelander more than this museum. Nothing reminds me so sharply that I'm not. When I met Þórður, I still held out some small hope that he knew something I didn't, that he could read the bridge of my nose or the shape of my hands and pronounce me found. Maybe if my Icelandic was better. Maybe if I could lay blood claim to my great-great-great-grandfather's Icelandic second wife. Maybe if I'd tried twenty years ago. Nonetheless, he was polite when we met. He invited me to sit down in a natty living room. He showed me some books he'd written that I couldn't read and a fan letter from abroad that I most certainly could. But the language yawned between us. We had so little to say. He said to call on him again.

SO, GO NOW, TODAY. AND IF YOU CAN POSSIBLY MAKE YOURSELF an Icelander before you get there, do that, too. In fact, do that first. Reach back in time. Rework those disadvantageous generations that somehow skirted this small dark island, unweave their strands and cast out until you catch these people in your net. Look with a surveyor's eye, and pull taut the line that runs through. But be quick about it. It's almost too late now. Indeed, I'm sorry—I believed it to be true when I put these words together—but in the very time it takes to tell you, it might have already become too late.

It was always true that we teetered at a threshold, but if we see it now, in high relief, it is perhaps only because Þórður is so very old. There is such anxiety. All these bonus good years are such a windfall, and surely we should be doing something right now to take advantage, because surely there is so little time left. Mark this: The first curator of *the second museum in Iceland* is still alive. And for as long as anyone can remember, not just that man but that *museum* has been Þórður. The two seem inseparable. Indeed, it seems odd to say "two," when they have for so long been more or less one. And yet, though we've been luckier than we have any right to be, it simply can't be that way forever.

If we're honest, the museum, the way one experiences it, is already not what it once was. Indeed, we may have lost that, lost the Þórður we are so ready to mourn, some decades ago. It's hard to say. We may have lost it last year and we may have lost it by degrees. We may have lost things we'll never know were once there for the taking. But because there is this one definitive reckoning on its way, emphatically inevitable even if statistically overdue, we find ourselves keenly aware, can see our loss before anything is taken from us. It's odd. We stand here now, every moment, waiting as if for a train, because we know it's coming, not the day when this museum isn't what it was, but a different marker: the irrefutable day when this museum can't be what it's always been.

But if we imagine a clean break coming, a reckoning, we'd do well to recall that such borders tend to be muddier, more porous than that.

The school in Skógar hasn't been a school since the last class graduated in 2000. There were only ever a hundred or so students at a time. Still, the school building remains where it always was, and like many school buildings for a long time in Iceland, it is still rented out as a hotel in the summer. The museum that started there is still kept close, now such an easy walk away that the proximity strikes me as reminiscent of the spread of suckering trees, the way they send out saplings from their roots. If you plant a tree, you'll get more trees in the same place.

Þórður lives in a cottage between the old school and the new museum with his sister, Guðrún, and her husband, Magnús. He has for ages. Guðrún was a teacher. Magnús kept the grounds. Þórður was Þórður. And the museum flourished.

Guðrún was museum staff for a while. They say she knows the place like the back of her hand. She's not identical to Þórður, obviously, but she knows the same songs. She knows the same people. She's read the same books. She's from the same place. Guðrún is ten years younger than her brother, and the way it's been, if he can't sort you out with the usual questions—Who are you? What are your politics? Of what people are you?—then she's the one to go online and find the genealogy there. She's the rest of the answer.

No one appears to notice. Only once do I hear her name. But she's been there with him the whole time. She's the other piece. That's what the guide says, after I've been hanging around the desk asking questions long enough. There is this possibility of grace. And still it seems we can't see her for what she is, even when we need what she might yet offer, even as we ache for a loss we don't yet feel.

ÞÓRÐUR WORKED FOR A TIME FOR THE NATIONAL MUSEUM, collecting folk music from around the country. It was winter work. I like to think you could hear that on the recordings, the whistle of a cutting wind, the dampening effect of snow piled up, some trace of the darkness calling everyone indoors. But we'll never know. The tapes were so expensive that to do the work you'd erase them, again and again, a palimpsest of silence after writing down the lyrics, setting down the notes. And if you think about it, even that silence is a kind of incomplete. Those are just the folk songs we didn't lose altogether.

At the museum, there was no restriction on what Þórður would accept. He'd add a German snuff box in with the rest just because it had been given to him. Indeed, after Þórður had collected the first two thousand objects, there came to him a single gift of two thousand more. Now the museum keeps three boats, a number of beams, a whole roof, and plenty of other stuff in storage, not all of it cataloged but maybe someday. Some of it will be wrapped in acid-free paper and forgotten. Most of it will never go on display. And still the collection expands, a breath that never exhales. Maybe it's no longer every week at this point, but there's still always something coming in, someone with something more to add.

I had taken the new ferry to an island off the southern coast, to see another museum started at a school and now freestanding, was there the first time I heard the National Museum of Iceland referred to as "the mother ship." Indeed, it is a museum so big it collects houses. It is a museum with both the power to lend and the power to absorb. The latter is a failsafe, a promise that any accredited institution might dissolve but that institution's collection will then be provided for in perpetuity, subsumed into the national holdings.

It sounds so generous to my ear: no object orphaned, all these pieces honored for all of us because some museum somewhere found them worthy. At last, a safety net in the lonely struggle to hold on! I would think this would be a great comfort to the professionals stewarding such institutions, but I've only ever seen it felt as a threat. These museums are already battered lifeboats. Their custodians have sacrificed so much for their collections that any talk of losing them is yet another insult in the consuming thrash and struggle of keeping a small museum afloat, the anticipated indignity of *our things* forced to go somewhere else. It's not necessarily the possessions that resonate, but the possessing, the holding on to what was hers and mine and yours and ours.

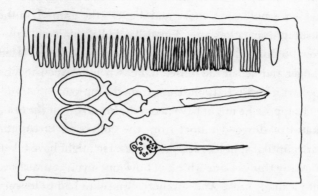

THERE HAD BEEN A CHURCH IN SKÓGAR SINCE 1000, SINCE
the official adoption of Christianity. It was torn down in
1890. That there is a church now, in the collection of buildings the museum has clustered together into something of a
village, a ghost town never lived in, is all Þórður's doing.
They say it was his dream to build a church. Of everything
Þórður's done, this is what he's most proud of. This is completely his work, this church. That's what the guide says.

For decades and decades, every time a church needed to
be renewed, Þórður was there. From all those bits and bobs,
he resurrected this church. He was at liberty back then to
go to the ruins of old farms, the old church places, the
graveyards exposed in storms. The farm of Stóraborg, one
of the oldest in all of Iceland, was at last swept away by
weather and the sea. Þórður started scavenging there in
1972. The archaeologists didn't arrive until 1978.

Þórður was born in a valley on this southern coast, at Vall-
natún, in 1921, at the foot of the Vestur-Eyjafjöll mountains.
When one of those not-so-dormant mountains erupted in
2010, it disrupted air travel throughout Europe for a month.

No one declared the island uninhabitable, but it was feared tourism would soon choke and die. On the ground, in the ensuing evacuation after Eyjafjallajökull's infamous eruption, Þórður had to leave just like everyone else there. He left Skógar and he left the museum, but when he evacuated, he took with him exactly one thing from the museum.

I suppose he might have taken the brass ring or the bone skates or dragged a boat from the collection across the earth until it split like sealskin shoes. He might have taken so many things—just think of how much you could shove into a single sack! And surely the museum had in its very collection some sacks suited exquisitely to this task. But Þórður was no Noah, and he left with no ark. He walked away from the museum unburdened except for this: a Bible dating from 1584.

These early Bibles are understandably rare, though their origin is rooted in proliferation. The first printing press in Iceland was shipped to a Catholic bishop in the north around 1530, and used for religious tracts and literature until it changed hands, when everything changed in 1550, and an ambitious Lutheran bishop set about production of the first Bible translated into Icelandic. As per the mandate from the Danish king, every church on the island had to contribute, had to chip in for the printing and promise to buy one of the Icelandic Bibles. This was a Bible that cost as much as three cows. It was a six-hundred-page volume in an edition of five hundred copies. And in its day, it was a thing of plenty, the Bibles not just sold but also given away to parishes ten or twenty at a time. I'm told some parishes still have theirs, even now.

That Bible, old as it is, did not strike me as the obvious choice when I first heard this story. It seemed odd that it was the only thing selected from a lifetime of collecting, one thing shielded from the unknown. When Eldfell erupted on neighboring Heimaey in 1973, the whole island, some fifty-three hundred souls, was evacuated within six hours. They were resettled by the time they went to bed. They took a minimum when they fled, took their photo albums, perhaps, but as the eruption went on for months and it became clear the Heimaeyians would be displaced for a year, or two or three years, as they had the chance to go back just to collect their things, they started to bring to the mainland clothes and housewares, the furniture they needed, and finally their refrigerators, everything of some sentiment, and then everything of use.

During Eyjafjallajökull's eruption, Þórður took just the Bible. And while it makes sense to me that he would choose it for its history, for its language, for its ties to the place, it makes more sense when I think of the Bible not as a holy text but as a personal object. Because this is a museum that makes me think of those first few pages of the family Bible, a museum that in its way acts like that place of record for all the births and the baptisms, the marriages and the deaths, those linking dates, marks made by hand and over years, that root us back and back to our own.

A MOUSETRAP IS A "WOODEN CAT." TO HAND OVER YOUR spoon is to die. This is because your spoon was so well made that it would last a very long time, could be passed on to your descendants. Except that the spoon was made of sheep horn or cow horn, and it bent, positively wilted, if the soup was too hot. There are things that linger in the language, the language a museum of its own.

Since Þórður retired, he's in the museum less and less. It

had been tapering anyway, his presence there, but now it's down to a trickle. You still have a chance of meeting him, your lottery shot of learning why this museum is personally, vitally, inherently *your* museum, the museum of your kin. But most likely, instead of Þórður, you get nothing. Well, if you're on a tour—and half the visitors are—then you get a guide. If you eat in the café, you eat the cooking of the women who live around here, who still know how to make dishes like in the old days. It's not nothing. It's just not him.

Museums, I am told, are not personal collections. Rather, they are the loci of scholarship and preservation, a matter of caring for the public trust and refreshing exhibitions. When they become a cult of personality, when they become the museum of one man, it sounds harsh to say it, but they've done something wrong.

They say Þórður is an authentic scholar, an autodidact, a collector of folk songs and the old ways and regional words for weather. They say he is a charmer, that all the ladies adored him, that he charmed them out of the things the museum needed. They say he's never married, never cooked his own meal. They say he's old-school like that. They say that's the thing about the collection, that he was considered really weird. "If you had another such crazy person in the east, you'd have another museum there." And yet, he wasn't the only one who noticed, who did something about one way of life disappearing, one way of life becoming categorically something else. How could he have been?

Iceland is now full of folklore collections. They are often the first museum or the only museum a town has. It's a kind of institution so well known to the Icelanders, its pattern so familiar, that its contents are not uncommonly dismissed as "the same thing from fifty different farms." They have become a thing of plenty. Maybe your town was like that. Maybe it had one of these museums, so enamored of its objects that it seemed enough just to hold on to them, carefully, assiduously, to privilege the things above their context, to assume the stories attached to them unshakable, like shadows.

"THIS IS A REMARKABLE THING. THIS IS RUBBISH." THAT'S what the guide says, in Icelandic or English or French or Italian or German or perhaps some other tongue I am forgetting. The guide is a costume designer or a prodigal son or a photographer from the Metropolitan Museum of Art. The guide is Tinna or Smári or Brooks. Each has their own way, and, as guides go, each is a flavor of perfection. Smári is a warm giant. Tinna is sharp and shy. Brooks is an outsider's insider, and when he talks he layers natural history and global politics and folk sayings as if lifting veil after veil to see this horsehair blanket for the first time for what it really is. When Smári stops to opine about bed boards, wandering visitors pull toward him like stray electrons, filling into shells encircling him, and then he moves toward old coins and the attraction pulls the visitors with him, vibrating. Oh, and when Tinna talks about the boat, sixty tourists restless from the bus fall quieter than an empty room.

This boat is the most important thing in the collection. That's what the guide says. It's the only boat of its kind, built to fish close to shore. Fit for sixteen rowers and one to steer. Fitted with thin oars and never a good time to use the sails. It's a boat like a Viking ship, the guide says, a boat that can be dragged to shore. And it's a beauty: broad and shallow, the wood that rich, warm color of a brandy cask. It was in service from 1855 to 1946. "That was a long time," the guide says. "This was a good boat." It's handily the biggest thing inside the museum, an upper limit, and the museum, once just a collection slowly filling a school basement, had to construct a whole new gallery to fit it.

The boat was retired at a time when the coast guard had incentive to burn old boats. It was law then: You couldn't buy a new boat without destroying an old one. That was the rule. A move toward modernization. A way of burning bridges with the past in a country that had so few literal bridges to begin with and, historically, so many more boats. If anyone noted that this move to modernize was an old one, as old as the burning of bed boards, the burning of carved Catholic saints, the burning of what scant scrub and trees had first covered this venting and volcanic rock, the burning of the shipwreck and the driftwood when it was better to be warm than harbor raw materials, they said nothing. They said it was better to sink the boat than drag it ashore. That was the wisdom, a Viking funeral without the corpse.

A boat may be built in the open air, but it isn't meant to live there. It expects to make one conversion, one shock into the sea. Pull it from its proper place in the salt water, return it once more to the air, and the transition makes it something it never was before. The wood dries and shrinks. The seals break their covenants. The constituent parts do not know where to swell and where to pull away, and the boat distorts itself until it cannot be put back in the water without sinking.

Of course this boat, this good boat, is settled now. It is going nowhere new. It is going neither back to the sea nor back to the earth, because it was left on the sand when it should have been burned. I assume no one had the heart to put a match to it. I assume they knew just how the wind and the sea would dismantle it, in time, all last traces of it consumed. Except then, instead, it was brought here.

The boat may well remain here for longer than the near century it sailed, all that time and not one life lost. And precisely because it was once a good boat, it is now something else. It is now a boat that cannot save anyone, that will bring in nothing from the sea. Indeed, it may remain always the way it is now: entombed in air, in a custom-built room, a kind of ship in a bottle, another sheltered curiosity. Or else it will be exactly as it is, no more and no less, right up to the moment it becomes something else.

THEY SAY IT IS NOT THE OPEN OCEAN ONE SHOULD FEAR, BUT the returning home. The approach is what's dangerous, the transition, where you can be dashed upon a rock in water still deep enough to drown. These are the places where everything absolutely has to change. These are the places where all can be lost.

For a long time a handmade shoe insert made a good courting gift. It would help you sort out your shoes from the confusion of uniformly mud-caked footwear at the church door, would sop up the damp, is heard still in the idiom "a gift under foot," meaning a present from a woman to a man.

There is a unit, always said in the plural, merkur, just for measuring the weight of babies.

If you take seconds at the table, you apologize for your greed.

And such is this museum. There is a skyr-tub, good to store food for three years, and Þórður himself restored the cow-tail filter. There are the chastity belts for rams, which also prevent disease. There are all the old books we do not read. And though the museum cases are cleaned every day and the eruption's been over for years, the volcanic ash is still falling, always. The ash, too, is on display. You can't see it except for the accumulation, but whether you ever see it at all, it is there nonetheless, endlessly, the ash still sifting through the air, still skimming the cases, still settling in thin, fine coats, to be wiped away again tomorrow.

This is a museum of old rituals, of daily chores, of things to do and things undone. This is a museum of kinship, of who we are by way of who we've been. This is a museum like music, like an instrument one man built and no one else ever learned to play or even dared take out of the case—if indeed it could have been slipped from its casing at all. This is a museum of scrap-savvy scavenging. This is a museum of wool and wood and blade. This is a museum of echoes, of abundance, a museum of plenty. This is a museum of never enough. This is a museum of what didn't burn. This is a museum of what wasn't washed away. This is a museum of precipice, of transition, of standing stock-still. This is a museum, now, of guides, of tongues you do or do not know. The guide says a lot of things. The guide says this in parting, as if handing you a whalebone beam: If you build a monument, you must be careful, lest you wall yourself in. This is a museum of what mattered, a museum pressed into your hand.

The Museum of Whales You Will Never See

There is a whale museum I suspect I will never go to. Once, I made it just as far as the entrance door, before deciding I'd rather watch the harbor, the clouds coming in. So I know it only as it's been told to me. I hear they built the massive room still too small to hold the exhibits. I hear they put a wall in the wrong place. There was a fire, a whale up in flames, and they never replaced it. They have no curator on staff. No scientists. If you know your cetaceans, you'll see that the shape is off, or the color, or the bend in the back. If you permit yourself a touch, you can squeeze them, these whales made of sponges, made in China. I like to imagine the whole museum of life-size whales shipped in a shoe box, each desiccated model touched by a drop of water and swollen, expanded up and out, bursting and unwrinkling into form, and suddenly a ballroom's worth of whales are over and above and around you, the total weighing no more than a suit of clothes.

My brother pointed out once, in a museum gift shop, how nice it is that there are so many things we do not need to own, that the bulk of their value is in just knowing that they exist. This museum is something like that. I so enjoy how it is talked about, the museum I imagine from the stories I have heard, that I cannot conceive of an actual visit there improving it. A friend of mine says why bother with this one in the first place when there's already a perfectly good whale museum in the back of a gas station, not even so very far from here. It is a modest display, so carefully done, and was made by the couple who own the place for no good reason except they took an interest, except they loved something enough to say it out loud so we might hear. It has heart, this museum. You would love it. If only you knew where to look.

I am always asking about this museum, but no one else has ever heard of it. No voice ever answers when I dial the number. At the bend in the road where it should be, there is a valley, not even more road. I stop in at the only building anywhere nearby, and it isn't really open. A dog barks and keeps barking. From this alone I should know I am not Odysseus, finally come home. Then amid the symmetry of four-top tables, their uniform white tablecloths creased just so at the corners, the woman who has come to hush the dog listens to my plea.

I keep saying "gas station" and "museum" and "whales." I draw them on my map, in the place where I've been told to look. I might as well be drawing dragons.

I show her the phone number in my notebook, the name of the road. I draw gas pumps and gas stations and display boards and whales. She nods and asks questions. I keep saying—because they are the only words that matter—*gas station* and *museum* and *whales*. Our progress is this: It seems the woman could send me to any one of these things, if only I would pick.

I thank her for her time. She puts a hand on my shoulder. She smiles as though she is pleased, as though this is resolved. She says good-bye and good luck and congratulations. She points and she nods and she waves. All this time and she has never turned on the lights. I worry she will linger at the dim window, will watch me turn back onto the road and realize that I've gone the wrong way despite everything she's said.

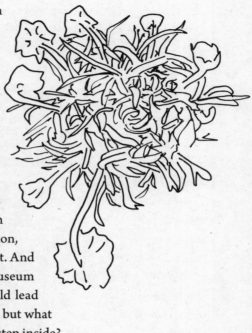

So now there are two museums I do not visit. There's a whale museum in the back of a gas station, but I can never find it. And there's a whale museum on the harbor I could lead you to this moment, but what good would it do to step inside?

THE END OF THE
WORLD

Herring Era Museum
(*Síldarminjasafn Íslands*)

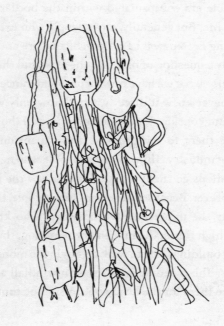

Herring do not jump unless frightened. Amid their many mysteries, somehow we have discovered this. We also know their activity is greatly controlled by the temperature of the water, though they range widely and their cycles are hard to grasp. We know that sometimes, when they swim, they leave luminous trails.

The Herring Years, as they're known, or else the Herring Era—now increasingly the Herring Era *Adventure*, for those of us too far removed to grasp that "Herring Era" alone should conjure intrigue and romance—lasted a lifetime. We mark the dates cleanly, from 1903 until 1968. It's long enough that a person could have been born and raised, gone to work and retired, been dead and buried without having ever known any different than the way it was then.

Or if your timing was right and you lived a long time, the math also allows that you might have seen all of it, rise to fall, a whole era encapsulated within the borders of your own long life. But generally, most people who experienced the Herring Era knew it as a diptych, a before and an after. It was only a question of ordering the feast and the famine.

Of course what we have now, in preponderance, are people who never knew it directly, who know only what they are told. But consider for a moment longer all those people who were there to see progress and expansion and the promise of industry. Think of those people who never heard the accordions go silent for good, never saw the buildings go dark forever. Because there were such people, those who knew only the unprecedented upsweep, who knew first-hand the high times, the machinery pumping, the workers crowding buildings safe to walk through, the money changing hands. These people grew up with windfall as a birthright, were there for the heady optimism, the tons of silver fish spurring on an industry—and never saw the crash. It's something to keep in mind, though they aren't here to tell us, though they, too, are all gone now.

DURING THE HERRING YEARS, THE TOWN OF SIGLUFJÖRÐUR was all mass and multitude. There were nine factories processing meal and oil, and it took 120 companies to process and salt the herring. The fish-meal storehouse was said to be the largest building in Iceland, and the chimney of the generator house, at 170 feet, its tallest concrete structure. There were hordes of foreign and domestic boats in the harbor. They talk about the masts, a forest of them, and piers like teeth in a comb. A walking tour of the harbor in its heyday would have been 4.3 miles, if you took the trouble to walk out to the end of each pier.

There were twenty-three salting stations then, and fifty to sixty herring girls at each station to process the catch. We say girls, but these were women, working outside the home, outside in the open air, metal tokens dropped in their boots and sinking down their calves as boys—and they were indeed boys—carted off barrels of their work product and made room for more. Before modern technology, all the guts they cut out of the fish were just thrown back in the sea. The shore was thick with fish oil, a tide of it, just as the yellow-orange aprons of the herring girls were slick with the stuff.

Siglufjörður was a town that, by itself, accounted for 23 percent of the country's export income some years, the lion's share of an industry in which all herring products nationwide peaked at 44 percent of export in the best seasons. Thousands of people were working. And for as long as the fish came to feed, the people came to work.

The fishermen stocked their ships and read the wind and sailed away from that northern coast, stayed away long enough to risk their lives in those North Atlantic waves. Before they had other instruments, other theories, the people followed the whales and the birds out to sea, in search of schools to weigh down their nets. They followed in particular the fulmars, those expert scavengers of fishing scraps that, in a twist of survival, have themselves learned to follow the fishing boats.

Birds have been hunting herring for millennia, watching their shoals from above. Herring spotting from aircraft became viable in the 1930s, and the nation's two passenger air carriers, the bookending Air Iceland and Icelandair, can trace their roots to those patrols spotting fish. Siglufjörður became one of the early towns to get electricity in Iceland, back in 1913, and to keep up with the needs of industry, expanded operations again in 1945, flooding a whole valley to do it. Farmers had to move. It was as if the sea had crowded in; places where you used to ride from farm to farm, now you rowed and rowed.

The herring were so important, they were sometimes known as "Iceland's gold" or "the silver of the sea." And the Herring Era was not unlike a gold rush, the flood of people come to make their fortune. I assume the word for it was *bustling*: the commotion on the docks, the musicians in the street, the women singing work songs, the dancing that sometimes broke out, all the artists come to paint. Sometimes the word is *cosmopolitan*—the mixing of people from different towns and countries, the increasing number of local boats never quite pushing out all the foreign ones. It was a land not of milk and honey but of fish and fish oil, succored not from the fat of the land but the salt of the sea.

*

WHEN WE TALK ABOUT HERRING, WE GIVE ONE NAME TO A thousand things. We mean always the jutting jaw, the spineless fins, the sleek silver bodies so likely to school in droves— but we also mean some two hundred species in the Clupeidae family, and other species, too, some of them relatives of the clupeids and some just look-alikes. The lake herring, you may know, is actually a salmonid.

We talk about toothed river and dwarf round and two-finned and red-eye herring. Middling thread and black-stripe and dogtooth and graceful. Pacific flatiron and West African pygmy. Hatchet and Panama. We say "herring" and may mean an equatorial longfin or a whitefin wolf.

There is no one herring, except in the word.

The word *herring* itself has uncertain origins, though it's tempting to derive it from the Old High German, from that ancient word *heri*, meaning a host or a multitude, presumably for their massive schools, but a good fit, too, for their array, not just their throng.

Herring are a lot of things. They are filter feeders. They are obligate shoalers. They are a fish of the open water. And they are a social fish—so much so, in fact, that they are rarely to be found in aquariums. Go ahead and look. They are so well adapted to life in a multitude that isolation, even a small company, leaves them fragile, both stressed out and sluggish, their hearts beating much too fast, and even the best aquarium cannot adequately accommodate their needs.

And no wonder. The North Atlantic sees herring schools of some three billion fish. Try even to imagine that. Stand out in the open, somewhere you can look up at the sky, where your vision is unimpeded unless it is by something the scale of a skyscraper or a mountain range. Look out and try to grasp the volume of three billion fish. That's almost five cubic kilometers of herring, and still what we call one school.

PEOPLE WHO LIVE IN SIGLUFJÖRÐUR CALL THE TOWN "THE end of the world." Yes, the roads have gotten better (paved or simply laid in the first place), and the tunnels certainly help, but even now it has that superlative isolation the nickname implies. At least, it does if you think in terms of land. But with respect to the wide and open sea, that same spot, that lovely north-facing fjord in the middle of the northern coast, is the beginning of everything. That is the geography that made Siglufjörður, at least in the Herring Era, the only place to be.

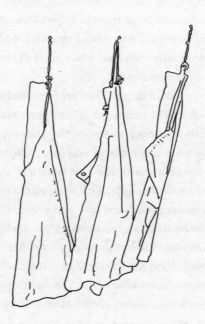

*

IN 1957, A GOOD FIFTY-FOUR YEARS INTO THE HERRING ERA, the town council of Siglufjörður was determined to have a museum. A heritage museum was their notion, and they elected a teacher, a trader, a principal, the mayor, and the town secretary to be its board. Because the idea for a museum came first, existed before there was any collection to shape it, they did not yet know, in those early days, exactly what kind of museum they would have.

The board hired a consultant from Reykjavík, and the consultant suggested they concentrate their collection on artifacts from the fisheries of North Iceland. This consultant might have taken an interest in the town's reputation for producing particularly adept skiers, because indeed it does. He might have walked the far side of the fjord and become keen on eiderdown, its weightless warmth, that gossamer fluff the eider duck plucks from her own breast to snug her nest of eggs, and that down plucked again from the nest to fill pillows and comforters and feather mattresses after the ducklings are gone. But there was such a din of commerce. Who could look at this center of industry then and not see to its fishy core? So it was settled. And a little later that summer, the museum, a museum of the fisheries, began to collect.

There are ways we like to talk of beginnings. We like "*Eureka!*" We like "Mr. Watson—come here—I want to see you." We like love at first sight and lightning strikes and an apple the moment it hits a head. We like the necessary, improbable flash. We really like the big bang. We like fate, but we like it all the more when it ignores the absolutely insurmountable and nonetheless dares to exist. And when I talk to the people who start museums, never do they talk about a moment like this. Not once. We can pinpoint the way a collection starts, the fact of the first thing, but a museum often enough has no one root. It is less discrete than continuous, less particle than wave. Its beginning is always hazy— no one thing, really, unless that one thing is something amorphous, something not really suited to words, something maybe spoken of best as something like *want*. These people knew they wanted a museum, even before they knew what kind of museum it would be.

WE DON'T KNOW WHY THE HERRING DO WHAT THEY DO. NOT really. We know a herring is more likely to have a full belly than an empty one when caught. We know they swim with their mouths open, expanded, so they might feed. We know they arrange themselves in grids when they swim, spaced neatly in accordance with the jump distance of their prey. What we don't know is how they pick their migration paths, why their routes change, why we can trace and model but not predict how they will thread their journey this year.

From Siglufjörður's perspective, 1966 "was a good year for herring." For the factories, it was the best, actually, the absolute peak. More herring than there had ever been. And by 1969, they were gone.

Not that they'd been raptured. Not that they went extinct. True, it had been an era without regulations—certainly not the way we know them now—and the technology had gotten so good, and surely the stock was overfished. There were still herring in the world, but they weren't showing up in the waters north of Iceland, gone from Siglufjörður and towns like it, though at first fugitive only from the north. The fish factories on Iceland's east coast still had steady work for a decade; some are up and running even now.

It was a crisis. To be sure, it was absolute calamity. The herring had been a rising tide and their harvest a sixty-year swell, a cresting wave, and then, just two summers after the zenith, a void. Informally, it went by the name, as if a plucky girl detective might solve it, "When the Herring Disappeared."

THE HERITAGE MUSEUM IN SIGLUFJÖRÐUR WAS, FOR A LONG time, more idea, more want than anything else. It was not exactly a thing disappeared, but it flickered in and out. Its board met nine times in the first nine years and then stopped meeting at all for the next eight. All the first two decades of the museum had to show were a handful of meetings and a score of objects collected. Yet in those eight years when the board wasn't meeting, the fisheries hit their summit. And in those same years, the fisheries collapsed.

In the beginning, the board thought they were making a museum of now, and before it was much of anything it had become a museum of then. Or else it wasn't anything at all really, except for a collection of twenty-eight objects stored in three buildings across town, a collection tucked away like a hope chest.

A COLLECTION OF FISH GATHERED TOGETHER IS CALLED AN aggregation. They need have no shared purpose. Indeed, an unstructured aggregation has a random quality, with any number of species and sizes of fish sharing one location but otherwise acting without relation to one another.

If that aggregation has a social dimension, however, if its fish relate in an interactive way, they are said to be shoaling.

You may know the noun *shoal* for its landform meaning, those ridges and bars and banks just above water or barely submerged, and it's the same word for these other formations in the sea, except with fish instead of grains of sand. Half of fish species shoal at some point in their goings-on, and a quarter shoal all their lives.

If the shoal is organized, if its members are synchronized swimmers moving at the same speed and in the same direction, identical vectors, only then are they said to be schooling. Schooling fish tend toward homogeny, are generally assemblies of the same species and, more to the point, fish of the same size and shape and coloring.

We don't know the exact reason for this rampant, unyielding conformity, but the "oddity effect" proposes it comes about because predators have an easier time targeting any fish in the group that is not like the others. Standing out goes against survival. And while you might assume a certain macabre utility in having a sacrificial lamb at the ready, really it's better for everyone, except I suppose the predator, to attract as little attention as possible.

The oddity effect also means that the juvenile herring, being smaller than their parents, form different schools than the mature fish, ever keeping like with like. Indeed, in their earliest stages herring are largely transparent. They are a floating bit of eye and gut in a body like a windowpane. They begin life nothing like they end up. And as such, despite their bloodlines, despite their manifest destiny to join the others at a later date, they begin life utterly unwelcome in the silver schools of fish they will become.

THEY SAY THE SIGLUFJÖRÐUR FIRE DEPARTMENT WAS exceptionally well trained during the 1970s and '80s. They had so much to work with. It was a town of timber buildings and timber piers, timber pilings and timber masts. It was a town built out to process something like half of the nation's catch. It hadn't been just full but packed to bursting—then emptied out, almost hollow. What reason was there for the workers to come if the herring didn't? There were all those people who just didn't come back; all those people who lived there, then fled.

When the herring disappeared, so many buildings suddenly lost their purpose. The town was filled with abandoned wrecks. The aging lumber wasn't maintained, would weather and rot. Wind blew through broken windows and gaps in the walls. The metal rusted. Joints weakened. Roofs collapsed. It was a matter of public safety that the fire department set so many buildings alight, let them burn, let them positively blaze, and then put out the fires they themselves had started.

Back then, "it was so ugly and dangerous." But it was something else unsettling: it was "our children longing for the time to leave." The old infrastructure had been heroic in scale; even forsaken, it was too much of the shoreline to escape, too close to the road to ignore, and there was just too much of it left standing to forget, no matter how much of what was left standing kept falling down. Maybe the locals would have learned to live with the disrepair, would have gotten used to it, if it weren't for what it cost people to live among the ruins.

It wasn't just the fact of it, a problem with the material world, of the way things splintered and shattered and broke. What it represented was worse. This was a place that could hurt you, just looking at it, a place that kept triggering the memories of sudden change, of total forfeit, of catastrophic loss. These people lived with not just the setting but also the symbol of their grief. More than a problem of place, it was a problem of memory, a kind of cognitive dissonance, of what it was to inhabit a grand old memory palace and watch it crumble around you.

In those decades after the herring disappeared, the town was filled with people who didn't understand why you would want a museum of this place at all, couldn't imagine why anyone would come to hear such a sad story. What would be the point?

SCHOOLING FISH ARE THOUGHT TO LIVE BY TWO RULES: Remain close to your neighbors. Avoid collisions with your neighbors.

I gravitate to the metaphoric value, the generally good advice of "Stick together and don't be a jerk," but the scientific value of the rules is that they describe how schools react in such stunning swift coordination, as if a school were not a collection of beings in the first place but all sum and no parts.

The two rules are sometimes modeled spatially as a matter of three zones, represented as expanding spheres, like the pulse of a sound wave traveling. The first circle surrounding a given fish represents too close. Think of it like the bubble of personal space in our own society, what's known as the *zone of repulsion* for fish, the space you want to keep clear or else collision is imminent.

The next circle, its radius a little wider, is just right, the proper amount of space to keep everyone in touch but not touching, close but not too close: the *zone of alignment*. The zone of alignment is how you pack a school together in a five-cubic-kilometer grid. It is the distance between you and your dance partner, close enough to read each other, but without stepping on any toes.

Beyond that, from the edge of alignment to as far away as the fish can sense, is the *zone of attraction*, the great, fat margin in which one fish, detecting another, will seek to get closer.

It's a Goldilocks description of the world: too close, too far, just right. It suggests a pendulum always pulling us to the center. And don't we want to believe in a kind of gravity ever drawing us into balance, into harmony and efficiency, into a position where we fit and a place where we belong? Do we not ache for it?

Truly, the zone of attraction is such a romantic prospect: its suggestion that it is enough to sense, to have some small trace of the thing we should draw near to. How tempting to believe that a mere glimpse could guide us, that flicker might bring us home.

But note that there is no name for that farther place, for the zone beyond, for the place past where our senses reach, and where most of the world is, most of the time.

IN THE LATE 1970S THERE WAS A FLURRY OF ACTIVITY, FROM one man, mostly, but with some friends to help, and after two years of collecting, these volunteers had a little exhibition in a little house on the hill, mostly pictures and the smaller things, the things that would fit. It was all very nice. But it had been only a decade since the herring disappeared. It caused collisions with the neighbors. It was still just too soon.

And so the harbor continued to decay, and the fire department dutifully continued to burn it down, and the museum wasn't much of anything. The cycle had almost run its course when, in the spring of 1985, there was a motion in city hall, perhaps in the very same room where the board for the heritage museum first convened. Only this time the motion was to tear down the last herring building, to be done with all that once and for all.

It was a popular measure. It seemed like progress, a thing they could predict. Or in any case, it seemed inevitable. At least it was something to do.

There was only the smallest of groups then, if you could think of them as that organized, who saw that their history had become invisible, knew that any other herring building left had already been altered or repurposed—a loose minority among the locals who believed it would have been shameful to let the last building go.

They had been trying to get this last building a historic designation, trying to raise funds to restore it and give the museum they imagined a home. But none of that was official yet. So before it could be torn down, these volunteers did for the old building what they had the time and resources to do: They painted it. They had no permission. The place was not properly theirs. But they claimed the old hulk with a new coat of red paint, and people saw it as if for the first time.

Maybe they didn't even see the paint. Maybe they saw only all the effort it took to paint it. Maybe the painting of one old, rotting building sounds superficial, cosmetic, such a minor contribution in the face of monumental breakdown as to put one in mind of rearranging the deck chairs on the *Titanic*, but this transformation was more than a makeover. Painting the Red House managed something foundational: It changed the outlook of the town. It demonstrated that the worst part of town could be restored, even if all they did was add a coat of paint.

Mind you, the Red House languished another four or five years after the paint job before it was serviceable, before it was safe, before it became the first museum building. But if what you want is an inflection point, a place where the shape of things changes, there it is: the painting of the Red House. It wasn't enough to have their memories, their experience, their language of fish and ships. They needed some further evidence of what seemed out of reach. They needed a vision of what had been and of what could be. It mattered that there was something they could see.

WHEN I THINK ABOUT THE RED HOUSE, I WONDER IF IT HAD to be the last building, if the volunteers couldn't have saved this one building until it was the only one left to save. Momentum can be hard to come by, and the last chance focuses the effort. There's a kind of urgency to the endling that's different from the last thirty, or even the last four,

then three, then two. So often we can't hold on to the one until we have lost the many.

There had been other houses, of course—I say "houses" from the Icelandic construction, *húsið*, for the way they so rarely translate a structure to the word *building* and so often tender the cognate *house*—but by the time the volunteers knew what they might want to save, most of those other houses were gone. In pictures, everything back then is ribs and timber, structures swaybacked and shrugged, bent like boat hulls, stranded like whales. The harbor resembles something part junkyard, part ghost town. If this was a place wanting, it was in the sense not of desire but of lack.

Red paint or no red paint, the whole first floor was rotten. One day, so soon into its reprieve, the Red House fell down like a house of cards. So they pulled it back up eight feet and shifted it over a hundred to build a new foundation under it. Then the volunteers left work one August day and a storm came in, and in five hours the Red House was blown on its side. The structure had a kind of stability before they got started with it, the way the wind could sail through its cracks, but once they began to intervene, once it started to become whole, once it offered some resistance, the old building got tossed around.

So many in town were convinced it was over then, sure the madness had ended. But the fever did not break. The volunteers had only to bide their time, to wait for the storms to pass, to wait until the next spring and lift the Red House up once more.

A HERRING JUST TAKEN FROM THE WATER IS IRIDESCENT, the oil-slick shimmer of green and blue and violet, but we don't think of it that way. The colors are so quick to fade in the open air, the herring soon a creature known not for its rainbow but for its flat silver sides. How practical for us to know it in this state, what it looks like when it's most useful to our purposes, the way we see it when the catch comes in. But how strange to mistake this as typical, to believe it is only the thing we see after we've pulled it from the water, and not a thing that lives there.

WHY WAS IT SO HARD TO CONVINCE PEOPLE? NOT JUST people, even, but eyewitnesses, the people who lived there, the very people who had seen the place in its heyday. Why did they need an intervention or an artist's rendering or a coat of paint when they could still remember, when they had the muscle memory of the work still in their hands, the old songs still in their heads?

It took twenty-five years after the herring disappeared to get enough distance to make this museum. That's a generation. And it wasn't just the residents of Siglufjörður; it took the whole nation that long to come around. It had been hard to separate the era from its absence, all that enterprise enacted at jaw-dropping scale from the yawning expanse of heartbreak in its wake. It's hard to say if they were too close to it—too close to the place and the time and the people and what happened—or if it was just the opposite: that they lost sight of its contours, had gotten too far away to see anything clearly, to sense it and draw near.

In 1991, a few years after the paint job but before the restoration of the Red House was done, the volunteers put up an exhibition. Mostly it was fishing equipment and things to do with the herring girls, some stencils to mark the barrel ends—nothing big, but enough to show they were serious about their vision for a museum and not just a bunch of

Quixotes out painting a building ready to fall down. And
for their next move, they made a brochure, not to show
what they had now or had had in the past, but what they
could have—what all of them could have—if they believed,
if they knew what to do with what was already there.

Örlygur was then the high school art teacher, a painter
in his own right, and one of the volunteers. Now, as I suspect then, he has a kind of gangly elegance, wears a sweater
so handsomely and with such good posture, you might not
notice the holes worn through the yarn at the elbows. He is
a man who will lead you to the last eider nest of the season,
will pour you coffee before you think to ask for it, is attentive to detail like that.

As a volunteer, he had been using his hands to shovel the
gravel and cinch the ropes and pull the nails out of old
boards, but for the brochure, he began to draw. The brochures were more image than text, his drawings used to
paint a picture of how it would be, how all of it would
change, the museum and the town and this specific stretch
of shore that looked hopeless if all you could see was the
way it was, all that actual lumber, so gray and splintered and
broken.

The volunteers took his drawings to the printer and
printed two thousand brochures, enough to make sure absolutely everyone in town had one in their hands. Enough
to make sure the bank and the politicians and the government officials giving grants had something to hold, something to look at so they could say yes. Which, more and
more, they did.

The museum now is staffed by Anita, the new director of
the museum, and Steinunn, the new manager of collec-

tions. They both grew up here. There's a picture in the archives of Steinunn as a little girl at the museum on a class
field trip. They are university-trained museum professionals, and they both say there was exactly one sentence about
herring in all their formal collegiate study of Icelandic history. I think about that when Örlygur tells me how the
translator who first worked on the museum text was married to a historian down in Reykjavík, and how the historian would look over her shoulder and ask, incredulous, "Is
this true?!"

At the museum's morning coffee break, Örlygur brings a
perfect orange to share, slices it open as fat clumps of snowflakes hit the skylight and melt. The old fire chief has come
for coffee, as he does most days, and another regular has
just read aloud the poem he wrote last night inspired by
this snowfall. A teenager who is summer staff has dropped
by after passing his driver's exam, is teased for how they all
suffered through him learning the accordion last year—
though later he will play it for me in the resonant arms of an
old oil tank they mean to use for small receptions, a metal
cylinder they've cut a threshold into because it had no door,
a thing rusting and echoing that holds the notes clear but in
haunting reverberation. All of it seems like a dream ful-
filled. But this orange is a revelation.

I keep thinking an orange has no business being here, at
the end of the world, in the middle of a snowstorm, in the
last November days before the sun sets behind a mountain
and refuses to crest again this year. I will not be here when
the sun comes back, when the town gathers together to
watch it happen, when the sun pancakes are sold, when the
children stand on the church steps with their drawings of

that celestial orb and sing it back into light. But I assume it is like this orange, precious and sweet. I assume all joy can be known from any one of its flavors. Perhaps all possibility.

Anita says: "Örlygur being an artist has made such a difference. He could draw what he was thinking, convince people." Steinunn describes it: "Like a fairy tale. He would draw it, and it would come to pass."

WE KNOW THIS, TOO, ABOUT THE HERRING: THEIR HEARING is excellent. And they can expel the air they've swallowed in high-pitched bursts to signal their location, not out of fear or famine but, it seems, because it's time to collect together and be still.

BACK WHEN THE VOLUNTEERS WERE WORKING ON THE BONE House, as the old fish-bone factory was known in town, they painted it, too—maybe they even used the paint from the Red House when they painted the Bone House roof red. But the Bone House blew over in a winter storm, and unlike the Red House, it never recovered. Not exactly. But its wood was salvaged to construct the factory building now on display: Grána, the old fish meal and oil factory, built from the bones of the Bone House.

Now the museum is a collection of five buildings open to the public, plus the oil tank for receptions. Now its buildings include Grána and Njarðarskemma: an old herring warehouse attached to Grána and presently concerned with exhibitions of electric power, plus a vintage spare parts garage and an antique laboratory to monitor the composition of fish meal and oil. There's also the Old Slipway, though it's not open from day to day.

Of course the museum includes the Red House, or

Róaldsbrakki, the one they painted in the first place, and finally the Boathouse, an experiment of its own. The Boathouse is the only one purpose-built, designed to look smaller than it is, to fit in among the row of other museum houses, though twelve vessels nonetheless dock within its walls: lifeboats and rowboats and harbor boats and purse-seine boats, all but bobbing in the air off the rebuilt pier.

And now there's the new building. That's what they call it, but the new building is not new. It dates from the late nineteenth century. It used to be part of a whaling station and after that it was a tannery, a concern for salting sheepskin, and from the latter incarnation it keeps its proper name: Salthúsið, the Salt House. It had to be moved, and now the Salt House sits in a cluster with the museum buildings that are open to the public, though it is being restored for the kind of work that happens out of sight: the mandate to register, preserve, and store the collection.

Making things last is an art form all its own in a place with such a short growing season, all those turf houses so ready to sink back into the ground, the sagas still on the reading list. Why else have a salt house, if not for the work of preserving? Where, too, are the smokehouse, the drying shed? Were not these always museums of a kind?

HERRING ARE A TENDER FISH. THEY SEEM SO FRAGILE IF YOU remember their scales are rounded, fall off almost at the touch.

THERE ARE SOME DELICATE THINGS HERE, BUT ON THE whole this museum has the advantage of being a collection of hardy, working things. As Steinunn says, "The museum has never been filled with glass boxes." Indeed, there's nothing to stop you from putting a hand on the machinery to feel the old paint and the metal grooves under your touch. There is a boat in the Boathouse you can climb up to walk the decks, or climb higher still and lower yourself down a ladder into working chambers almost too small to turn around in.

Síldarminjasafn Íslands, The Herring Era Museum of Iceland, is now the biggest maritime museum—and in fact the biggest industrial museum—in all of Iceland. Örlygur says, "This is a museum that started as a place, was a place before it was any one building." There were so many herring villages and towns throughout the north and east of this country. Theoretically, any one of them might have made this museum. But as Örlygur says: "Other towns, they threw everything away. Maybe there's one or two buildings they don't know how to use. It's the same things here, the same smells as their towns, but here these rusty, smelly things are now gold."

Many people think Örlygur is a collector. It's not how he thinks of himself. He's an organizer, he says—that's the word for it—one to make order of chaos. "Maybe the best works are organized," he posits one morning when we are talking about painting, about thinking, about how anything gets done. I find I tend to agree. At least, that's how I often think of writing, as a matter of organization. It is not a problem so much of finding the right words, but of how to arrange them. And of course what to leave out matters as much as what to include.

When the volunteers started to collect, they collected without curation. There wasn't time. The material history was already falling apart. It had already yellowed and crumbled and torn. It was rotting or molding or collapsing. It had been thrown out, abandoned, and discarded. They collected to combat both entropy itself and the increasingly systematic plans to dismantle and forget. They collected as though they thought it might all just disappear, without warning, like the herring.

Perhaps it is misleading to say that they were collecting at all. The point then was not even to collect so much as to intercede, to gather up everything that might be relevant while there was anything left to gather. There was no filtering of what really mattered. No one was terribly concerned that iron and wood have different needs, different coefficients of expansion, that iron rings rust and the rust is bad for the wood, that a barrel or a boat is ever at war with itself, and that you simply can't preserve boats on land under a bare sky like a stone. The point was only to have options, later. They could define the collection, later. They could sort it out, someday, later. But if there was going to be anything they might want in the future, they had to claim it, now.

Once they got going, what factories were left cooperated, gave them allowance to take what they needed. Machinery and more came from Ingólfsfjörður in the Westfjords and Hjalteyri in the north. But of course it wasn't just an industrial issue. It was personal, too. They began to get phone calls. There were so many phone calls. "People tell us they have something we might need," is the way Örlygur puts it. "We were so aware of what we had lost. We must take this. Keep it and then rethink it later."

They wanted to see a forest, and so they gathered every tree. With this mind-set they saved whole buildings. And they saved the scraps to make other buildings whole again. They saved bunk beds, and barrels, and hooks, and tins, and everything they weren't sure they would have the chance to say yes to again. They saved a fleet of ships. They didn't save everything, mind you. Of course they didn't. Of course they *couldn't*. But they said yes enough to fill up ten buildings to the rafters, to the gills, and hoped that what they needed, whatever that was, was in there, somewhere.

THE HERRING THEMSELVES ARE A COLLECTION. A COLLECTION both massive and highly organized, elegantly stacked in their grids, rank after rank, as far down as the eye can see, if you lean over the boat to look. They come to the surface most often at night, particularly when the water is calm, and while they don't feed in complete darkness, they will feed in faint light. They take their prey by what's called a "definite act of capture." I love that phrase. How decisive. How discrete. As if anything could be so perfect. As if anything could be complete.

IT'S BEEN A LIFETIME SINCE THAT EARLY MUSEUM BOARD first convened and began to collect. It's been a good forty years since the volunteers intervened. If that first phase was notable for its precious few things, the volunteer era was neither restrained nor austere. This was collecting as salvation. This was scooping up whatever might be relevant so someone else in the future could decide what mattered in the past. There's something sort of humble about it, really. I love the humility that someone else might know better, the trust that someone else could get this done, the utter faith that someone else might love the thing we love.

Some things are ruined from the wait. Some things are worth keeping as props, or for decoration when they put in a café someday in the future, but they aren't what you'd accession into the museum collection proper. It can be hard to tell what matters. As Örlygur notes, "We're talking about ordinary things, not precious like Picassos. We are very poor on special things. But we have so much to remake this world."

They have the pieces to remake a world—they have the witnesses to check their work. There are herring girls who aren't even old women yet.

Guests come to the museum and recognize things from their childhoods, from their grandmothers' houses. And it's not just Icelanders, but people from Denmark, Norway, Russia. It's been nearly a half century since the herring disappeared, but if you think about it like Steinunn does, "Nineteen sixty-eight isn't that long ago. People still have those things in their homes. Then people die, and those things come here."

LEGEND HAS IT THAT THE FISH OF THE DEEP ONCE CAME together and named the herring as their king. It is easy to imagine them, the swarm of their congress, the pageantry of their decree, the utter solemnness of their undertaking, and the way the light filtered through the water to illuminate these delegate fish of every shape and hue. But it took me some time to make sense of the symbolism, of what the herring king could possibly mean.

For starters, I do not generally think of kings in the class of things that can be chosen; it seems generally in opposition to the whole project of royalty for the subjects to have a say, though a neighbor once told me as we sat on her porch how the people of Norway did just that, and not so long ago. They didn't exactly take out an ad in the paper—NORDIC COUNTRY SEEKS REGENT—but it wasn't unlike that, either, the way they found a Danish prince and made him a Norwegian king. And once, at Lisbon Sauerkraut Days in Iowa, a man walked out between the flaps of a beer tent to crown my partner and me with bottle caps, as he declared us the king and queen of dancing.

The king snake is not king because it is the biggest or smartest or whatever passes for most noble among serpents. It is king because it is a snake that eats other snakes. But the thing about herring is that it is an excellent bait fish, preferred over all others in some places, though they themselves seldom take a bait hook, if indeed they ever do. Herring are not individually selected like that. They are fished as they live—in quantity, in a mass.

If the herring is king of fish, I suspect it is not because it is most beautiful or most populous or controls the most territory, but indeed because it feeds so many other fish. It is predated by any number of seagoing species, keeps *them* alive, feeds so much of this watery world while the herring themselves swim with open mouths. The herring is king, I suspect, the way bread is holy.

THE ONLY FACTORY STILL STANDING IN SIGLUFJÖRÐUR stands empty, shuttered one hundred years after the first factory was built in 1911. Its machinery was recently torn out and sold to some concern in South America. Perhaps the machinery has a new life there. The old factory does nothing at all, for now, but echo.

Once that factory falls or is torn down or the fire department burns it to the ground, it is unlikely there will ever be another at the end of the world. Unless you count the boats, which themselves are like factories these days. As the museum text observes: "By the end of the 20th century, a single herring vessel could, in one fishing-trip, bring ashore as

much fish as three small ships caught in a whole fishing season in the early days." Herring was a summer occupation
back then. Museums, too, used to be that way. So much
used to have a season.

When the herring disappeared, people fled. Now the
same people come back, and they can't believe it: their
hometown beautiful again. It used to be if you still lived in
Siglufjörður, if you were from there, maybe you tried not to
say so when someone asked. It used to be maybe you left.
Anita says, "Today we joke about Siglo expats becoming
the biggest fans." The locals who left now attest that the
food tastes better in Siglufjörður than anywhere else, the
weather is more temperate, and you will never be more
handsome than with a haircut from the local barber.

All this because the volunteers took something that locals saw in a negative light and managed to make it positive
again. What's remarkable is not the transformation, but the
restoration, the recovery of what had been there the whole
time. This is not spinning flax into gold. It is no conversion
of water into wine. As Steinnun says, "We see it best in people still bringing us objects. Now it's worth something." Or
rather, it's worth something *again*.

Just this summer, "someone tried to give us a stove from
a boat. It was old, made in Iceland. But do we need a stove?"
This summer a man cleaning out the loft of his parents'
house uncovered a fisherman's rucksack (very rare); a herring girl's apron, still covered in fish oil; and a stack of newspapers. The man called the museum. "Do you want this
stuff? Or should we throw it away?" Those were the options.
It used to be the museum always said yes. Now they have to
decide.

ONE OF MY FAVORITE THINGS IN ANY MUSEUM ANYWHERE IS
here: *Artefacts of the Herring Era, Washed Ashore 1994–2004.*
It is a collection curated by the sea. There are twenty objects from those ten years, hooks and tools and such, affixed
to the weathered boards of the Boathouse wall in such an
arrangement as to create the shape of a herring—though
you'd need to take another two steps back, mind you—two
steps off the lip of the walkway and into thin air—to see the
shape and know it.

Remember how the Icelanders, for a while, named them
"diamond herring" and "God's gift"? It was not enough to
name them a multitude. They were something even more.
That little fish the capelin has also been good for Iceland's
export revenues, but it is not half so storied as the herring,
is not said at the very least to have been the foundation of

both the Dutch and British empires. Surely it has made some kings, too, but no one says as much.

And anyway, mackerel is the new thing. That's what I hear. They started coming five years ago. Maybe they'll stick around so long that there will be Icelanders who cannot remember a world without them. Or else, these things happen so fast, maybe they've fled. Maybe it's already too late to say yes to them. Maybe they're already gone. What is there in this life, in this world, that doesn't disappear? What is that most distant, precious thing we can, if only faintly, sense?

The Museum of Darkness

I f you cannot imagine the terror of trees, what understanding can we share? You must be shown. And here, in this black harbor-side house, in the new exhibition, in a space enclosed like a closet but with room enough to traverse a winding wilderness path, you'll see. Because it's all well and good to talk about the emigrants, about the Icelanders who could not face another bad winter, another bad summer, and so ended up somewhere like North Dakota. We can show you the old letters. We can show you the old slates and desks and the stuff of one-room schoolhouses, but you will not understand the foreignness of North Dakota, how downright spooky it is to leave a mostly treeless place and then find yourself in a forest. At night. Eyes glittering at you from animals you do not know. It is the darkness, yes, but a kind of claustrophobia, too, a danger that pens you in.

The people in North Dakota were very generous; they had lots of old things, and when the museum director returned to Iceland with a crate full of foreign artifacts and frontier props, he was prepared for inspection. He had everything in order. He had documented the furniture and the maps and the raccoon skins. He tried to get somebody's attention.

"Don't you want to see what's in the cases?" he asked.

"That's all stuff for exhibition?" the customs officials volleyed back.

The director nodded.

"Then we'll see it when it's on exhibition," they said, and he passed through with his crate.

If he told them he was bringing in a forest, if he told them what he'd packed was fear, if he told them there was darkness in those cases like they'd never known, they couldn't have imagined it anyway. They couldn't have stopped him for that.

ON NECROPANTS

The Museum of Icelandic Sorcery and Witchcraft
(Galdrasýning á Ströndum)

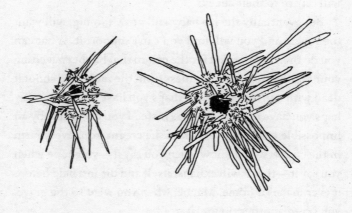

f you are poor, you have options. You might begin to collect strands of hair from a virgin. You might weave those strands of hair into a tiny net and drag it through the sea. And when you pull from the sea a sea mouse, twitching in your net, you will make a deal. The sea mouse released into servitude. The sea mouse thrown back in the sea but returning to you every so often, dripping, with lost coins in its clutch.

Or you might dig up a body. Rob a grave for a rib. And bind that rib with twine and say the right things and make yourself a rib baby. The rib baby, you should know, is voracious. At first it will be satisfied with a few drops of blood pricked from your finger, but it will grow. You will score your flesh to make a nipple of your thigh and it will suckle there. Which is fine—which is fair—because the rib baby has been stealing cream for you. Every night. The best cream. Nicking it from the neighbors while they sleep. And for a while this cream will nourish your children. The color will return to their cheeks.

But eventually the rib baby will grow too big, will want too much, and you will find you can't support it. What can you do then but thank it for the cream that has been feeding your family, look at it breathless from the raids, and shoot it dead with a silver button? Perhaps you have no button. Perhaps you have no gun. Perhaps instead you give rib baby an impossible task: send it to skim the cream from every farm in the country. You know when you say it—you hope when you say it—that it will exhaust itself and die in a field before it ever makes it home. Maybe, when you went to the grave, you saved another rib for later.

Yes, it is wretched to be poor, to sleep on sheets washed once a year in a turf house with one hole to vent the smoke from the hearth and the room crowded with sheep penned in for the winter. But perhaps you have a friend. Not a friend, but a man. A man who agrees, of his own free will, that upon his natural death you may flay him. From the waist down. Tan the skin and sprinkle the solution and say the words. If you've done it right, you will step into his skin. Your foot in his foot. Your calf flexing his.

I cannot tell you for sure about the fit. Sometimes, I imagine the necropants as a second skin, a skintight skin you could forget was not your own. Sometimes I am convinced they would require a belt. Or suspenders. A rigging of some kind to keep them up. No one dwells on whether you wear them under your regular pants or in lieu of them, because the point of this is wealth. Poor as you are, you will find yourself in want. And reaching down, dipping your hand into the scrotum like a change purse, you'll retrieve a few coins. Do not be greedy. This part is key. Don't go rooting and scratching and digging around for all you can get. Trust in the necropants. There will be more lucre. Take just what you need.

But, whatever you do, don't die in the necropants. That would be bad. Like burning-in-hell bad. You don't want that. What you want is someone who wants an endless groin bank but without the effort of flaying anybody. You want an heir. You want someone who will step into the left leg when you step out of the left leg, step into the right leg when you step out of the right leg. That's the thing about the necropants: You cannot take them off without someone else taking them on. Not to dry-clean or air out or mend the rip in the knee. There must always be a wearer. Someone is always responsible. But once you've made the transfer, once you've settled someone else into their skin, it is done and the necropants are no longer your concern.

*

THERE IS NO MUSEUM OF POVERTY. NOT PER SE. NOT IN Iceland. Not in a country where there are no tracks and no wrong side of them. Not unless you count the turf houses, or the folk museums full of things from the old days, the poor days, the scraping-by scrap days, whole centuries of days in the smoky dim foul of cod-liver-oil lamps while all the whale oil, clean burning and bright, was shipped south and east to illuminate Hamburg and London.

But there is, out in a remote fjord, the Museum of Icelandic Sorcery and Witchcraft. It doubles as the tourism office. There to greet you is a man petting a cat. They've recently added a restaurant. And though outside in the streets it smells like fish, inside it smells like cookies.

Twenty years ago, there was just the tourism office, and its goal was to help you find your way back to wherever you had meant to visit before you lost your way and wandered in here. Hólmavík's hospitality then comprised a grill at the gas station and a little hotel in the stone house, though let it be said that the stone house had a great cook. Hólmavík was a far-flung hamlet of four hundred souls. Then, twenty years ago, a group of people came together wondering what they could do for the place.

THE CAT IS MR. HIPPOPOTAMUS. HE IS APPROPRIATELY LARGE and round and gray, and seems as comfortable at the museum as anywhere else. At the juncture of the room's functions as gift shop and restaurant and tourist information, high on the wall behind the cashier's counter, there is an oversize portrait of Mr. Hippopotamus staring beneficently into the middle distance, what Sigurður Atlason calls his communist leader pose. Sigurður Atlason is the man petting Mr. Hippopotamus.

In interviews, Siggi gives his title as Sorcerer. Or, sometimes, Chief Sorcerer. It would be accurate to call this man Manager or Cofounder or Head Chef or Chief Storyteller, but Sorcerer better suits the spark in his eyes and the ruddy weather of his skin and the finger that does not end in a fingernail and the wild silver-flecked hair smoothed under a felted wool hat that tapers to a floppy felted wool tassel.

Sorcerer is what he tells the American college student who has a video camera and "just a few questions." He says the same to the Basque film crew that has come to talk about the Basque massacre and the monument to it that the museum recently erected in the courtyard. "It's the worst thing we Icelanders ever did," Siggi says to me about the 1615 killing of thirty-two Basque sailors.

There's a name for it in Icelandic: Spánverjavígin, the slaying of the Spaniards. It may console you to know it's the last documented massacre in Icelandic history—indeed, the only mass murder the island can remember. Fourteen men were killed one day, eighteen more a little later, all of them murdered a month after most of the crew survived the September shipwreck of the boat ready to take them home.

The Icelanders were not whalers, not unless you count the scavenging. "Hvalreki," they say: May a whale get stranded on your beach. The Basques, however, were hunting all across the Atlantic. In Iceland they paid taxes for the privilege, paid also to disembark and process their quarry on dry land, paid to collect the wood to build the fires to melt the fat into oil. They weren't bad visitors. They were known to sell the meat cheap, at times even give away the smaller whales they'd harpooned and brought ashore. They bought things and traded things and had enough to say that four lexicons of the era record a burgeoning Basque-Icelandic pidgin. The problem was only that they paid their money to the Icelanders, not to the Danish crown. Certainly this was not a problem for the Icelanders, who were maybe the poorest nation in Europe at the time, but it was a problem for King Christian IV of Denmark, who not only owned Iceland, but had war chests to fill and witches to burn and was in the very royal position to decree things.

And so in the first few months of 1615, with the Icelanders in their fourth notably terrible winter in a row and starting to starve, the king decreed an end to their interactions with the Basque whalers—no more trade. But as a consolation prize, the Icelanders were now legally entitled to attack the Basques, to take their boats and their goods and their lives.

That fall the boats were already packed to sail home for the season, but then there was a winter storm, one so bad that even ships in the harbor were not safe, were smashed together and broke apart and sank.

If you are shipwrecked in a starving country, there is no sheep to sell you. The eleven whales that should have made your fortune are scattered now—their meat eaten, their bones built into houses, their oil spilled back into the sea.

What wasn't lost to that storm were three whaling captains and their shipwrecked crews. Captains Aguirre and Tellería gathered their men and took to longboats, traced the coast north and east until they found a ship to take them on. We know they found passage from there. We know nothing of them after that.

The third captain, Villafranca, took a different route, found no such safe harbor, lost fourteen men who were hacked to death while sheltering in a cabin, lost the rest to a different mob, their eyes stabbed, their ears, noses, necks, and genitals cut—"mutilated, defiled, and sunk in the sea," wrote Jón Guðmunsson at the time. Villafranca himself was pleading with a priest in Latin when he was struck with an ax. He then ran into that sea, where he swam, like a seal, like a fish, like an angel if it were not feathered but finned. He swam singing. He was singing a beautiful song the Icelanders did not know could be sung, so beautiful, singing until his pursuers rowed out to him—still swimming—and a stone knocked into his head and the song out of it, his body pulled into the boat and stripped back on shore and eviscerated, and only then, standing up to fall down, did he die.

The memorial to Villafranca and his crew is outside the museum, on the harbor side. It consists of a stone set with a metal plaque's worth of text, framed by a set of cetaceous jawbones curving to embrace two driftwood logs and a square stack of bricks. It was dedicated the last day of winter, which in Iceland came at the late date of April 22 that year. And at the memorial's dedication, Westfjords district commissioner Jónas Guðmundsson took the opportunity to finally revoke the order, until that moment still technically on the books, that Basques in the region could be killed on sight.

"The worst thing we Icelanders ever did." Siggi says it and looks out to the sea. The worst thing, he says. This in a country where a man was once sentenced to death for muttering an incantation to make his sheep mind him better.

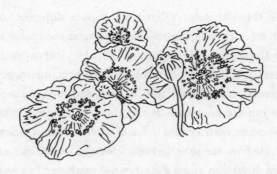

Not even an incantation to make them the best-behaved sheep you ever met, mind you, with table manners and curfews and the courtesy to hold the door for you as you pass—just sheep that minded *better*. Yes, this from a man who spends his days enmeshed in a history of Icelanders choosing to immolate each other.

IF YOU HAVE A BIG ENOUGH PROBLEM, YOU GO TO YOUR LOCAL sorcerer. Should that prove insufficient—if no one else can help—well then you upgrade to a Strandir sorcerer. That's the gold standard. It's basically fail-safe. Only once did a Strandir sorcerer ever fail to get the job done—an issue with a lake monster in the east—but happily there were still the Sami people to appeal to, back in northernmost Europe, and though even they cannot totally rid you of your lake monster, cannot banish this giant writhing worm, cannot bind it bodily to the bottom of the lake, they can at least tether it, tip and tail, so that only occasionally does some section of its middle surface, and far rarer still is that surfacing so much as sighted. The solution is perhaps imperfect, but it's much better than it was. You could almost forget that the monster is there.

Strandir is a region on the eastern edge of the Westfjords. The road that goes through it forks just north of Hólmavík, hugs the coast, and dead-ends at the thermal baths of Krossneslaug. Strandir was for a long time very inaccessible, with no roads going anywhere, and laws that would cost you your life if you dared trade with the foreign ships sometimes sailing past. If it has been congenial to any transportation, it is as the beaching shore to much of the driftwood that spends years, sometimes a decade or two, floating from Siberia, seasoning in the currents.

Even now, in peak tourist season and modern times, a bus connects to Hólmavík from the south no more than five days a week. Three days a week, a different bus company on a different schedule will link you to points north. The denizens of the Strandir region don't think of themselves as a strange, closed people. They do not think of themselves in magical terms. But if magic is not a part of their identity, it has long been a part of their reputation. Historically at least, other parts of the country would talk—about *them*, about their famous sorcerers, about how people from Strandir always win in athletic competitions. Amazing! What good wrestlers they are! Too good, if you think about it . . .

IT COULD HAVE BEEN WHATEVER ELSE—A WHALE MUSEUM, or whatever. In 1995 Jón Jónsson wrote a whole report on the potential for tourism in Strandir. But when it came down to it, this group of people in Strandir was interested in folklore, not in the sense of things passed down but in the sense of tales told. They thought about the local stories. They thought about the distracted trolls caught in the first rays of the sun and turned to stone. They thought about the seal-headed woman bent on revenge. They thought about the sorcerer calling in the fog to make his escape.

This first group, Héraðsnefnd Strandasýslu, was a collective of Strandir's local governments aiming to benefit individuals throughout the region and to provide visitors with access to cultural heritage and entertainment. From them we get Strandagaldur, a nonprofit institution that tasked itself with "research[ing] the image of Strandir as the home of Iceland's sorcerers, the period of witch-hunting in Iceland, and to communicate this to the public." It took a few years, but in 2000 they opened the Exhibition of Witchcraft and Sorcery, and they govern it still.

Oh, it was a struggle in the beginning. The subject of sorcery and witchcraft touched on religion, and there was pushback. There was talk on the radio, for instance, and statements from the church. But for the would-be founders of the would-be museum, the real issue with the content was not so much ideological as material. "There was nothing you could put your fingers on," Siggi says. These were people who wanted to tell about things they could not prove existed. And so they stumbled upon a particularly Icelandic problem: how to display what can't be seen.

This is a problem also with the Sea Monster Museum, and the Museum of Prophecies, and any of the Saga museums, and certainly Icelandic Wonders, a museum of ghosts, elves, trolls, and the northern lights. When it came to sorcery and witchcraft, there were at least books and court records and written descriptions to work from. "It is possible to show an invisible boy," Siggi reminds me one day in the gallery. "In fact, it's easy," he continues, stepping to the side with a flourish: "Here he is!"

WHAT WE KNOW ABOUT THE MAGIC, WE KNOW FROM HAND-written books, copied in secret and kept hidden. Grimoires, they're called. Having one in your possession, even just a few pages, could have led to a death sentence. Or, if not your death, the pages burned under your nose while your body is flogged. There aren't a lot of grimoires known to exist, and the ones we have were copied late—maybe only a few dozen altogether. Some survived as curiosities in foreign collections; some remain in Iceland. Of the ones we don't have, some surely disappeared along with the crew and the king's antiquarian and his chests of manuscripts and the boat taking them all to the royal port in early seventeenth-century Denmark, lost along the way and never heard from again.

The most common feats in grimoires are of love magic: To banter with somebody. That men will love you. A stave to get a girl. And, sure, to make a horse go lame or to win at playing cards or to calm anger or to call up a northern blizzard, but it's probably to get a woman, that a girl will love you, to make a man and a woman love each other, that a couple will never divorce. So maybe you send flowers. Pass a note. *Carve these staves in your palm with your saliva while fasting and then shake hands with her.* The human condition, as read in grimoires, is a fundamental pining.

Theft is the second most popular topic: To know theft. To get back what has been stolen. If you want to prevent theft from your house. If you want a man to steal something. *Put this stave under the horseshoe when shoeing the horse and stealing it will be of no use.* Note with how many variations you might prepare a washbasin so that in three days' time you may look upon it and see the face of the one who stole from you. It seems so singularly benign: the desire for economic security, not in the form of amassing untold riches but of simply not losing whatever is yours. This is not waiting for your ship to come in; it is plugging the leaks so that the ship doesn't sink first.

SIGGI IS NOT A COLLECTOR. THERE WAS THAT TIME HE KEPT a belly-button-lint collection to disturb his daughter-in-law—which proved effective—but with objective achieved he abandoned the project. Siggi has a background in theater. He'll tell you he came to Hólmavík as a teenager for a summer job and has yet to make enough money for a return bus ticket. Or he'll tell you he's really a carpenter who accidentally went into theater, spending a few years directing around the country before falling into a parliament job. The latter was "bad work, horribly paid," but at least it prepared him to apply for funding for the museum.

"It seems like everything has led me to this," Siggi says to me one afternoon. It is true that he seems singularly suited to his work, that it's hard to imagine the place without a sorcerer in chief. But by another accounting it's a pretty standard curriculum vitae in a country where everyone wears a few hats, where you have a job but also a start-up or a novel or a band, and if you don't like work at the hospital, then why not farm organic produce and open a bed-and-breakfast?

Siggi is wearing a black chef's jacket over a T-shirt with a fraying collar, has a gray goatee with two days' stubble, and his hair is pulled into a short ponytail under the felted mauve hat with a traditional hanging tassel suggested by an untraditional felted strip. He hands me a fleece blanket so we can talk on the picnic benches outside. The view takes in the Basque memorial and the parking lot and the harbor no boat ever seems to enter. There are flowers on the tabletops. There's an old recliner out in the sea air, parked next to the little greenhouse growing lettuce for the restaurant and the sweetest, most perfect thimble-sized strawberries you ever put in your mouth.

There in the courtyard, Siggi tells me how he thought it would be good to have a fence. Well, not a fence, but a division between the courtyard and the parking lot. Anyway, he asked around and a friend brought stones, set them upright at intervals, to bound two sides of the museum building and protect the picnic tables and the greenhouse. They were already installed, rough gray stones in gray gravel every six feet or so, when Siggi first counted them: twenty-one. Like the twenty-one Icelanders burned at the stake for accusations of witchcraft, he noticed. That's when he started affixing markers to them, one for every death. He hadn't meant to make a memorial when he went to make a fence, and now the marked stones also enclose the Basque tribute, two memorials radiating out as you exit the museum's side door.

It's the coldest summer in thirty years, and sitting outside, Siggi is wrapped in gray wool, warming his hands around a cup marked with the stave to make invisible, while a brown spider picks its way across the loose weave of the wool. Sitting opposite on the picnic bench, I drink coffee from a cup with the stave to find a thief, cut it with milk from a cream pitcher marked with the stave for necropants, watch the spider make its way.

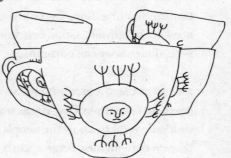

*

IF YOU ARE ILL, IF YOU ARE GASSY OR FAINT OR WEAK WITH
flu, you have options. Herbs, mostly, what we have are
herbs, but also mouse droppings and fox brains and cat
meat and human fat. Alcoholism, as you know, is cured by
drinking infant's pee. Mix bird droppings with the spit of a
fasting man, rub it on your skin, and you can forget about
those spots that have vexed you so!

Or, you might instead try magic. It's so much less inva-
sive. Maybe not *you*, delirious or feverish or unable to move,
but someone looking out for you could carve runes, draw
staves, could mark a board or write on paper or bake over a
fire or trace with blood or cut into metal—could make it
better, could press the words and the symbols to your fore-
head, slip them under your bed, lay them flat against wherever it hurts.

Most charges of witchcraft in Iceland had to do with
someone else's illness. Indeed, six of the twenty-one Icelandic burnings are connected to one sick woman, and a seventh to her sick daughter. So often in these cases it is sick
women, sick girls, sick wives, that it seems "sickness" must
be code for "pregnancy," yet I find no sources to support
this, and contemporary accounts seem unabashed in report-
ing children born out of wedlock or the occasional sexually
transmitted infection. Certainly, there were enough other
ways to be unwell. Goodness knows we continue to live
with ailments we can't diagnose.

THE MUSEUM IS OPEN EVERY DAY OF THE YEAR. "YOU CAN
come on Christmas Day, if you want," Siggi tells me, and I
suddenly want to know the people who do. In an afternoon
there you might meet some cyclists, a couple on their honey-

moon, an international set of Viking reenactors fresh from a show in Reykjavík and popping by to say hello to Agnes's granny in the little handicraft shop next door. Indeed, the Viking reenactors tell you, before the little shop was set up two years ago, Agnes's granny was in the same spot but in a tent, and "it is not very nice to sit in a tent all summer, and now there's a wooden door to close against the wind." Once a comic maker left the museum saying, "I am a comic maker, and I will make a comic about this." Three years later, Marc Védrines's trilogy, *Islandia*, arrived in the mail, with the museum thanked in the dedication.

Only a very few tour groups come. Siggi says it's better that way. A busload of forty people is enough to fill up the space, and anyway it's better to go at your own pace, not rushed to make the bus. The museum is free for visitors under age fourteen, so every kid in town comes and goes as they please. Maybe there are school groups from other places. But they, too, are not so common.

Back when the museum had only summer hours, visitors who found it closed just called to see if it might open. The hotel would call. It was so sad to shut up everything at the end of the summer, and Siggi found he was in the building most days anyhow, so at some point he just stopped locking the door. Then even more people came. But what to do with the people who came? They needed things. The town's restaurant closed in the winter, for instance, so the museum opened a place to eat. And a whole party would leave if the menu couldn't accommodate a vegan or a seafood allergy or a locavore, so the menu expanded until there was a local mussels platter and baked fish and meat loaf and seafood soup and a vegetarian masala always served in the dedicated green masala bowls. No, it wasn't enough to have a museum—you had to provide services, which just made it easier for more people to come and need more things. "And so," Siggi says, plating a chocolate cake, "you begin chasing your tail."

TECHNICALLY, THE MUSEUM OF ICELANDIC SORCERY AND Witchcraft is not a museum. Or it is a museum because it translates itself as a museum. In the early publications it called itself an Exhibition of Sorcery and Witchcraft, but anything that was created by some third party, such as the tour book entries and the articles, had a habit of listing it as a museum. After a few years, the Exhibition of Sorcery and Witchcraft stopped fighting to correct this. Trying to preserve the name was just causing confusion. People heard *exhibition* and thought it was temporary, called to ask if it had already closed. Or else people sometimes heard *exhibition* and sometimes heard *museum* and, assuming they were two different things, were unclear on which one they were trying to visit. So, poof! Give the people what they want. Why shouldn't it shift its shape? It is a museum if you speak English, but in Icelandic it has always been Galdrasýning— literally a magic exhibition.

There are thirty-seven words for magic and sorcery in Icelandic. They range from full-on supernatural intervention to the mere sleight of hand of a card trick. A synonymous selection is stenciled in all caps and red paint on the black outer walls of the museum: *gerningur, galdrar seiður, kukl, ákvæði, fordæðuskapur, fjölkynngi,* and so on like a spook house. It's arresting, the paint as if the walls would bleed, and the words themselves, as they weather, as if the blood was scabbing over. I have several hobbies in Iceland. I like to survey how tall an elf or hidden person would be, were these mythic creatures to choose to reveal themselves. I like to confirm in every new town that there is one street, the first street the town ever had, named for the harbor or peninsula, and then one that comes later, with the automobile, that second street named the Icelandic equivalent of Main. I especially like to ask, "What did this building used to be?" It was always something: a factory or a dance hall or a municipal shed. A private home, perhaps, or a movie theater.

The Museum of Icelandic Sorcery and Witchcraft used to be a *pakkhús*, a kind of hardware store plus shoes and feed and fertilizer. When the *pakkhús* operations moved locations, the city used the old building as a shed. Further back, in 1928, it was not even one building but a pair of houses, and where the exhibition starts now was an alley. Iceland has a way of keeping on with old houses, of finding new crabs to live in these shells. Inside, you wouldn't think of the time when it was two, but the outer structures show their history: one half concrete with corrugated roof, the other wooden walls with a turf roof added by the museum and currently a little patchy, some mushrooms taking root.

IF YOU ARE SUSPICIOUS, IF YOU ARE NOT AS RICH AS YOU might like, if your wife has mysteriously taken ill, you have options. Because surely this illness is the work of evil, and not plain malnutrition or rations gone bad, but magic, specific magic, invoked by a human being. You know that family new to town? That guy who's been here forever but no one likes? That mother and son? You know that Dane who keeps proposing to your maid or what they used to say about his dad? Well, let them prove their innocence, if innocent they are. And if they aren't, if they cannot find twelve peers who believe them when they swear it, if they are then sentenced to burn, well, perhaps you won't object to inheriting their possessions, in recompense for all you've suffered at their hands.

If witchcraft was one route to financial gain, and a dangerous one at that, making an accusation of witchcraft was itself another. At least 170 individuals were accused of witchcraft in the Icelandic courts. By Magnús Rafnsson's count, a third of those cases were brought for causing illness; another third, for having or using magical staves or signs. If mere possession of a magical stave or sign strikes you as a trifling matter, the thing to remember about Lutheran orthodoxy in seventeenth-century Iceland is its focus on God's will, especially the acceptance of bad things, which are God's punishment and are actually good things in the sense that we might be saved through them, though they will be terrible to endure. The problem with magic is that it endeavors to intervene. Striving to influence the world is either your shot at survival or a catastrophic failure of faith in God's will. Why not sit still and pray and be thankful?

All in all, a quarter of these cases were acquitted and a quarter of the accused flogged. Another quarter of the outcomes are unknown to us here at this late date, though they may well have repeated the kinds of events we do know about: how some individuals paid fines, while others were outlawed and cast out. We don't know how many people died just from the whippings, which could be scheduled in phases, extending your capacity for suffering by giving you time to nurse your wounds before inflicting them afresh.

The court records tell us about sentencing, but they don't account for the aftermath. They pay no mind to the mortality rates of ostensibly nonlethal sentences, to what happened if you were pushed too far or an infection took hold or you otherwise never recovered. *Carry this stave on your breast, on the skin of a heifer or on sanctified paper, if you have to defend your case.*

KOTBÝLI KUKLARANS, THE SORCERER'S COTTAGE, WAS BUILT as a companion to the museum and dedicated to the poor tenants of such dwellings from the seventeenth century. It's a turf house, the turf cut in four different ways, each cut of sod considered a different type of material and used for a different purpose. This cottage now, like those cottages then, is in a constant state of repair. Inside, a crossbeam carved with a stave has fallen loose on one end and hangs cantilevered over the hearth. Siggi pushes on the beam, tests its give like a child working a loose tooth.

After summers of work spent constructing it in the first place, the cottage opened in 2005 at Klúka in Bjarnafjörður. It's fifteen miles from Hólmavík and the museum, but directly adjacent to the Hótel Laugarhóll. Both the cottage and the hotel overlook the hotel pool. There is no town there. There is the hotel and fog and hot springs and green land.

Strips of bark wash up with the driftwood. They dry in ribbons and prove easy to light. Siggi kindles one and tosses it into the cauldron. It is a sweet slight smoke. There are other visitors, but no one in the cottage seems to mind that we have started lighting things on fire. "It smelled better than the animals," Siggi says, motioning to the part of the room penned into stalls to house the sheep all winter. Also, he adds about the superior smell of the smoke, "Better than you." Which is surely true in a time when you washed the bedding with the ammonia of human urine aged six months to be your cleaning agent. It would have been horse urine to wash your hair, and no reason not to use it warm.

IT WAS THE DANES' IDEA TO BURN THE WITCHES. I THINK WE can all agree they started it. Sure, fine, maybe a few Icelanders brought the notion back to the island, brought it back with their luggage and the educations they received in Copenhagen because there was no university in Iceland. Probably that's it. Colonizers, you know. Maybe, fine, we *acted* like Danes, but it was a temporary madness. We can still be proud. Only twenty-one people in a thousand years killed for being witches. Only one of them a woman! Our witch burning is not the misogynist kind you've heard so much about, not the rampant indiscriminate burning by people plump and drunk with power and fear. Our witch burning shows restraint.

And we won't dwell on that, on whether Icelandic women register so lightly on the persecution meter because we *so respected* female empowerment here that there was no impulse to stigmatize and subvert it, or whether it was because the weaker sex of this weak nation had not even power enough to make us fret. Perhaps we simply know this: A woman would not come up with necropants.

THERE ARE NO ARTIFACTS LEFT. NOT IN THE MUSEUM. There's a complicated genealogy of dead witches and their rich relations spread out under the peaked roof upstairs. There are some old books in other archives, foreign libraries. There are court records somewhere else. The museum has made up for the lack of necropants, the lack of rib babies, the lack of sea mice and the nets to catch them, with facsimiles. It is a very visual place. A gray-robed corpse breaks through the main gallery concrete floor as if from a crypt, and the rest of the facsimiles fit each in their private alcoves, warmly lit, ringing the room like stations of the cross.

The necropants are to scale, life-size. Their texture and color reminiscent of nothing so much as the flap of fake vomit we got from the joke store as kids, but then the legs rolled around in dryer lint to approximate something like body hair.

I am fond of the glass in museum cases, the way you can catch your own reflection overlaid on an object so that at just the right angle you appear to be wearing on your own head the same glittering Mycenaean crown you cannot touch. The necropants are installed too high up to achieve this illusion, exactly. You appear to be wearing them up to your chin. Perhaps like the thigh nipple and the invisible boy also in this room, here it is better to use your imagination.

There are nineteen text panels and eleven installations in the main gallery. Ten, if you fail to count the invisible boy. Fewer still should you elect to discount the parchments and books; the pan, the broom; the rather hideous scorn pole; or the four monstrous rib babies and the butter churn.

"Here," Siggi says, pulling out the wiggle of willow branches tucked in the corner display. "Whips like this! I was telling you." As he holds the branches, we both stare at what is essentially a six-foot log with irons, propped against the wall. "This was hard," he says about getting the irons. "Getting these rings, getting them right." The museum had hired a blacksmith to make the iron collar on a chain, the iron cuffs pinned by a massive nail driven into the wood. "And so expensive," Siggi says, almost to himself. Indeed, they couldn't afford the leg irons to complete the set, though the restraints would have been there, the legs immobilized as surely as the arms and the neck while the willow branches beat down across the body.

Siggi tells me that it was hard, back in the day, to find a person to wield the whip. Historically, you might be asked to whip people until they were almost dead—their backs shredded raw under your hand—and this would be hard enough, but even if there were some bloodlust in your soul, such a deed would mark you. Even if you needed the wages, you could hardly afford the social cost. No, not even the professionals, the judges and jailers, could be counted on to carry it out. So, sometimes, there was a bargain: If you were a person charged with some lesser crime, you could serve your sentence instead as the whipmaster. A bargain: a day or two of work for your freedom. Your freedom to leave, mostly, because while you wouldn't be formally cast out after that, you'd have to go start your life somewhere else, somewhere people could stand to look at you.

"HERE WE HAD TO CREATE EVERYTHING." THAT'S WHAT Siggi says. Emphasis on the "we." For instance, the woman in the photograph posed with her rustic skirts hiked up and showing a thigh nipple fit for a rib baby—she works across the street at the municipality. There's no telling where the rib baby resides. The necropants model, however, lives over by the Sorcerer's Cottage, and had to stand still for eight hours as the latex set. "But you know," Siggi says gently, "the delicate parts were made by hand."

The invisible boy is the son of a local farmer. "Maybe there are footsteps in the sand," Siggi says, gesturing to the bottom of the vitrine. "Maybe those footsteps are his."

It wasn't meant to be like this. The exhibition was designed to change. Everything you see should have been switched out by now, the objects standing in for the unseeable themselves dismantled and put away and disappeared. But the inventions are proving permanent. The very first day they opened the exhibition, it was such a hit that they knew they would never change it. The museum has expanded the hours and published three books and added the restaurant, but in terms of the exhibition, here we are, just the same, fifteen years later.

THE SEA MOUSE IS REAL, BY THE WAY. *APHRODITA ACULEATA.* Not a mouse so much as a worm, buried head-down in the sand some two miles under the sea. It's the size of a harmonica, with a bristly comb that's fluorescent in life, the color drained away to brown-gray in death.

A few weeks before the exhibition opened in 2000, Siggi had a flight delayed, stopped in at a Keflavík museum to pass the time, and discovered the creature. He hadn't known. The whole time they'd had the old words, the old stories, they hadn't known to attach them to a thing still living. Nor had the curator at the Keflavík museum known the folklore. The two men were so very glad to meet, to complete the knowledge the other had lacked. Siggi had nothing more to offer after the tale of the enriching sea mouse, but the curator had

a spare specimen, gave the sorcerer a sea mouse of his own. So Siggi carried it with him, on the flight to Copenhagen and back again. The same sea mouse you see here in the case.

YOUR CHILDREN WILL PLAY WITH SHEEP BONES AND SHELLS as their toys. There's no harm in that. There's not much else to spare. The leg bones represent horses. The jaws are cows, the toothy ends tapped into the earth as they graze. Somehow in death, in play, the sheep's bones are not its own; only the sheep's horn represents an actual sheep. And a seashell is not some sea creature but a dog, rounding up all your sheep.

When your children grow too old for bone toys, they may instead keep with them a bone from the sheep's ankle joint, the vala, invoking its powers of prediction, nodding to tip it off the crown of their heads and then bending to read whether it lands showing an affirmative convex bump or the concave hollow that means no. Maybe at church they see a whale's rib among the beams. Maybe at home there's a whale's vertebra worked into a bowl. Maybe you grew up the same.

The thing about bones is that you'll be tempted by their power. Specifically human bones. Especially the teeth. Maybe to cure your wife's toothache, maybe to make a rib baby—one day when you've run through the alternatives, maybe you enter the church graveyard and dig up someone you know, a stray Englishman or your old nanny, unearth them with all due respect, because nothing else has worked, because otherwise you are at a total loss, because their bones may serve you yet. Because there is so much you need, and only so much you have.

If you want the edge of your scythe to remain sharp, if

you want to put a man to sleep, if you want to ease the ene-my's anger, if you want somebody to lose his way, if a cow milks blood, if you want to hide something. If anyone hates you. If you want to be good at wrestling, if you want to win debates. If you want to do evil to somebody. If you want to turn magic against somebody, if you do not want the cap-tain to catch fish. To change somebody's disposition, to make sheep tame, to damage a horse with a man riding it. To get your wish, to get the thing you crave, to get what you ask for. That no one will see you. Against fright of darkness. If you want a favorable wind. You have options.

The Museum of Obligation

Samúel Jónsson was born in 1884. They say the man never had money in his hands until he retired and drew a pension. And what he did with it, immediately, at age seventy-two, was buy paint and brushes and bags of concrete, because what he wanted was to make art.

He painted landscapes. He sculpted figures. He painted an altarpiece and gave it to his local church. Imagine all those years, nearly a lifetime, that he sat in that church with his private vision of what it all meant. Surely that vision evolved. Surely it was fearsome and awesome and terrible, each in turn. And then, one day, he made that vision physical, material, something separate from himself, and arrived there where he dreamed it as if returning it home. Only the church didn't want it. The church would not accept it. So Samúel Jónsson made his own church, and erected the altarpiece there.

I love this as a story of undaunted independence, of artistic freedom, of doubling down, of sticking it to the man. But there is a way of telling it that is all about obligation, a telling that is almost meek. Samúel Jónsson had made something holy. And when a holy place would not take it, he was obliged to find it some other sanctuary. The nature of the object demanded this. There could be no other way.

I say church, but it is technically a chapel. It's on his farm at the end of the peninsula. The chapel is made of concrete, its architecture inspired by Russian postcards of great churches crowned with onion domes. If you've come this far down the gravel road, if you're careful, you can open the chapel's red door and let yourself inside.

Indeed, Samúel Jónsson made not one but two structures, one early and one late, the pair accompanied by a small menagerie of his painted concrete sculptures. The sculptures to be seen outside include, at more or less life-size: a swan with its cygnets, a seal, a human figure feeding a seal, a human figure with its hand held up as if to wave or shield its eyes, something like a massive blue seahorse, and a semicircle of six lions radiating out like a setting sun and backed up to a white chalice of a fountain as if holding it up with their rumps, no two tails the same.

After the artist made his chapel, he made a museum. He made a museum to hold the things that wouldn't hold up to the weather. He made a museum to hold the things it takes a special effort to see. The museum doesn't have hours. There's no one there on staff. The day I went, we could not get in. This is the second structure. Perhaps it is a twin.

Standing there, in the shadow of the museum, between

the valley and the cliff-edged coast, my companion told me
about coming out here as a boy, coming out with other kids,
the way the old man would show them how to add water to
the fountain—like this—all those children on their tiptoes
between the lions.

NUDGED INTO
THE SEA

Icelandic Sea Monster Museum
(Skrímslasetrið)

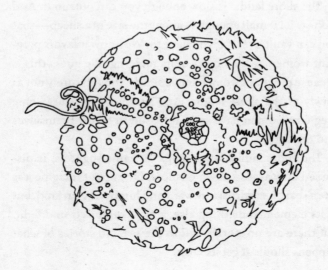

I've often thought about what it could have been.
But have never reached a rational conclusion.

—KRISTJÁN PÁLSSON

It looked a bit like a whale. Except it wasn't.

—ÞORLEIFUR JÓNSON

The shore laddie, deep within its sea-monsterly heart, wants only this: to nudge you into the sea. We don't know why. We don't know what happens next. Perhaps it wants only for you to register the shock of cold and wet shoes. Perhaps it wants you just to feel the waves against your shins. Perhaps it has come to guide you home, to a place you never knew you belonged, beneath the depths. Perhaps you have gills that awaken in the water. Perhaps this is what's best.

The shore laddie is slow enough you can outrun it. And anyway it is small enough—about the size of a sheep—that you can vault over it if you have to. We know it favors pregnant women as the object of its nudging. We guess this is because pregnant women move slowly, though surely not as slowly as the shore laddie. And surely not because some pregnant women have special reason to throw themselves into the sea.

The shore laddie, as perhaps its name suggests, is discussed only as it's known onshore. One might imagine it is like a seal or a walrus, awkward and lumbering on land, but in its element something else, a mass of muscle and fight. But there are no stories of it in the sea. No stories of what happens should it get its wish.

It sounds so singularly ineffective, the shore laddie's mode of attack, so charmingly benign. How utterly unthreatening the shore laddie is, how minor the malice of this creature who at its most alarming, at peak fearsomeness, attempts only to nudge you into the sea. You want to pat it on the head.

Other monsters are all threat and startle and terror. They invoke the unknown, the sharp and unexpected, the way everything can be gone or lost or broken, unrecognizable, in a moment. This monster, on the other hand, is almost cozy, persuasive: a monster that sidles up, tucks in, sort of G-rated and so gentle as to seem almost kind. It sounds like a thing you could tell a child about, without undue distress, when her father doesn't come home.

But the thing that most deserves your attention may not be the massive beast flagged by a fiery red mane, rocking your boat, spitting poison, scalding you with steam. It may not seem like an immediate threat. Who even registers this tenacity, the doggedness by which it aims, by degrees, to sway your course? Its persistence is so easy to discount, its press against you surely a thing you can deal with later.

EVERYWHERE IN ICELAND IS SOME KIND OF REMOTE. IT IS almost always a word I reach for when describing a place here, though I mean it differently every time, the variables of far away and hard to get to and minor road and edge of the world always in novel combination, the mountains this time higher or the wind sharper or the tunnel finally open.

Bíldudalur is remote in the way of things cut off. The mountainside is steep and tall, and both the sun and the moon struggle over the crest. The gas station is the restaurant is the grocery store. If you attempt to arrive by public transportation, it is convoluted and expensive and will take the better part of a day. If you take the advice to hitch-hike, the route is an open jaw and you pay in uncertainty and time standing in the cold and fleeting rain. It's only a generation ago that Bíldó was a place where the coast guard fetched you from boarding school, one fjord over, to bring you home for Christmas. Or maybe you took a boat to visit relatives for the New Year and the weather intervened and you couldn't come back until Easter. It was 1980 before the road could be kept open all year round. Even now it's ninety miles to reach Ísafjörður in the summer, and more than triple that to make it there in winter. Occasionally, in the summer, there's a flight that lands close enough to tempt you, connecting only from Reykjavík, with a descent I've heard will drop your stomach in your mouth.

Even people in Bíldudalur don't talk about Bíldó so much as they talk about the fjord, Arnarfjörður, in which the town is set. The fjord is six miles wide and nineteen long, which is big even as fjords go, and named for the first settler here in this chunk of the west-facing side of the Westfjords, that old craggy antler of land that extends from the northwest corner of the island—though it is so ancient, old as the country's eastern edge, that we should perhaps say the island extends from it.

Though it is also known for eagles, the locals tell me, "Arnarfjörður is Iceland's most notorious monster fjord." It's home to at least four of the nation's sea monster varietals, as great a concentration as anywhere on the island. The monsters seem to congregate in the deep water there, not unlike the whales and the shrimp more commonly found.

The fishing quotas started thirty years ago. At first they

limited the fisheries. Then the quotas were sold. And often enough they were sold away from the people who lived there, who had always fished there, who had always depended on that catch. Eventually a few concerns owned everything worth having.

If you lived in a place like Bíldudalur, if you knew it well enough to call it by the shorthand, Bíldó, then the quotas were sold away from you, consolidated in other hands, bit by bit, deal by deal, until the town you knew growing up dwindled from 400 residents to 120. Indeed, by the year 2000, you probably didn't live there at all. You couldn't sell your house, because there was no reason to move there, but by the same token you couldn't stay. "It was really bad—no jobs, people moving. If young people went away to school, they didn't come back. For many, many years, there were no jobs."

Starting in 2003, though, at the end of June in odd-numbered years there was a town festival. Town festivals didn't use to be much of a thing in Iceland, but there's been a rise of them since the 1990s. Enough so that now, if you play your cards right, you could attend a different festival every weekend for the whole summer, filling up on fish stew in Dalvík or lobster soup in Höfn or raising a pint in Bíldó, the batch brewed just for the occasion and a new label designed for it every odd year.

The village was founded in the nineteenth century to fish cod and help keep Spain in bacalao, but it was later known not for growing but for canning green beans— Bíldudalur's green beans, hence the Bíldudalur's Green . . . Festival and the phrase to ask about it: "Are you going to the beans?"

*

IT'S NOT HARD TO FIND SOMEONE IN ICELAND WHO HAS SEEN a ghost. There are plenty around to tell you about scrapes with the hidden people. But the monster stories, the sea monster stories, are kept close to the vest. Their tellers are often distinguished by their age, not because they have lived long enough to see one, not because things were different in the old days, not because it takes a lifetime to hone the storytelling skills to do it justice—but because they have reached a point in life when they simply don't care what people will say. We can all agree there are ghosts. But see a monster and you might be crazy.

Þorvaldur Friðriksson is a news editor for the national radio station. He has been following monster stories for some time, and in his odd hours at the station would call the old folks' homes, working his way around the country, home by home, to ask if anyone had a monster story to tell. And lo, sometimes they did. It startles me every time I think about it: all the people we don't listen to, enough or at all, the staggering silence, and all the things we might hear, if only we would ask.

Þorvaldur was brought up in

the Westfjords, the son of a lawyer and book collector, and well trained in natural history. He found fossils. He tagged birds with ID rings. An arctic tern he registered was found twenty years later, dead, in the same spot where he first found it. He went to Sweden to study archaeology. Once he started calling Iceland's homes for the elderly, working the map, slowly circling the country, he might hear ten or twenty stories in a day.

He's quick to point out that stories from 1700 and those from the 1920s describe the monsters in the same way, that as recently as 1900 lake monsters were there in the recognized zoology. Then nineteenth-century Icelandic writer Benedikt Gröndal started penning articles asserting that monster claims come from the stupid and the uneducated, and we don't see written accounts about the monsters from 1900 until the 1960s.

Þorvaldur has spent twenty years collecting eyewitness accounts of monsters—"maybe hundreds, maybe a thousand." He says Iceland has three active sea monsters and three lakes each with different creatures. He says one in three people in Arnarfjörður can tell a story and aren't ashamed to do so. He has sat with eyewitnesses to sketch the monsters they remember. He coordinated with a captain to send a U-boat down more than one hundred yards to take pictures of the craters there. Lake monsters leave tracks, you know. Perhaps sea monsters, too.

IF YOU START WITH THE FIRST COMPLETE MAP OF ICELAND— Abraham Ortelius's from 1585—note that it is famous for its facts. It is so careful with its place names, its topography, that it is sometimes said only an Icelander could have made it. To be sure, Icelandic bishop Guðbrandur Þorláksson prepared much of its information, but Ortelius was Flemish, still known almost half a millennium later as the father of the modern atlas.

And if you doubt the ability of Ortelius, geographer to the king of Spain, to see a place he never laid eyes on, then note the driftwood gathering on the edges of his Iceland, and the polar bears—just "white bears," in the parlance then—never landed but clustered on floats of ice in the northern sea. Note the volcano Hekla raging. Count the whales, the narwhals, the walruses, all the creatures measured in that ancient unit *ell* but nonetheless identifiable, even if you have never heard of this unit that is roughly the length of your forearm, even if you would draw them all differently now.

We have records of monsters in Iceland as early as 1345. Or even earlier, from the sixth century, if you trust Saint Brendan the Navigator, if you believe he made it from Ireland to Iceland and back. Ortelius labeled the creatures in his Iceland's waters with letters from A to Q, keyed to explanations that don't fit on the map engraving proper. It's easy to find fault. Sure, orcas don't hunger for human flesh or stand a whole day upright on their tails. We have absolutely no evidence, at present, that walruses sleep twelve hours a night dangling from cliffs by their tusks, but it had been the going wisdom for centuries when Ortelius printed it under letter N. Nor did he know what exactly a sperm whale was, but make no mistake—he knew we'd been carving chess pieces from their teeth.

Say what you will about the sea hog or the sea cow or the sea horse. Think what you like about descriptions of whales with no teeth, whales as big as islands, whales protecting fishermen in fights against other kinds of whales. Doubt, if you must, a fish covered with bristles or bones. Reject the cliff-dangling walruses, surely not there by their own efforts but hung like Christmas ornaments by the hand of God! But Ortelius wasn't wrong about the amber-colored blobs of ambergris, not vomit but something like it, a cetaceous by-product we still add to perfumes—a fixative, traces of it on your skin right now, perhaps, evaporating from your neck.

Ortelius is the first person we know of who articulated a theory of continental drift, of the Americas torn away from Europe and Africa through a succession of earthquakes and floods. The division he was describing was something entirely too big, too long ago, to be seen on any kind of human scale, but with or without the tools of direct observation, of having been there the whole time, the pieces fit. It was there at the edges. One had only to study their coasts.

THERE'S A RED BUILDING IN THE HARBOR THAT USED TO house three families, then one, and now it's just a summer house. It's called the Rams' House, from even earlier in its history when it was full of rowdy young workers. There was a time, even longer ago, when the town had been bigger than Reykjavík. Back then it had its own currency.

Meanwhile, in 2007, Iceland was being called an economic miracle. The residents say, "These were crazy times. Spending and spending! So optimistic!" The economy had opened in the mid-1990s, and tourists had flooded in. There's a story I am told not infrequently about those early times, about tours organized from abroad specifically to witness the Icelandic women, so famously beautiful, in their native habitat. I have yet to corroborate it, to find the flyer or the ticket stub or the tour guide that would give it the flavor of fact. Which perhaps is why it strikes me as a kind of monster story of its own: these creatures one might hope to see, unobtainable, marked as other, perhaps not just beguiling but also bewitching, powerful in ways we don't understand. Certainly, the hidden people are like that: taller and more attractive and richer than we are.

In 2007, there were enough former Bíldó residents now living in the capital that they had what amounted to an informal club of expats, a satellite, a group of Bíldudalurians who got together near their new homes in Reykjavík. And as often as not the conversation turned to what they could possibly do for this place they'd been forced to leave. Even in the boom, Bíldó showed no signs of bouncing back.

That year at the beans, the band played, the beer had its new label, and the news editor was aboard a boat leading a monster cruise down the fjord. He was telling the stories. There were so many to tell, and so many people on the boat leaning closer to hear. It was a hit, and not just on the boat. "This was in the news two days in a row. The television news."

The response was too big to ignore. For all the time they'd been asking what they could do for their hometown, they suddenly knew. They founded the Monster Society in Bíldudalur a few days later, convened it over the phone. And the point of the Monster Society, from the very beginning, was to start a Sea Monster Museum.

THE SHORE LADDIE IS THE SIZE OF A PONY BUT WITH shorter legs. It's been seen grazing with the sheep. Þorleifur Jónsson was trout fishing when he spied one not ten meters away. It had "canine teeth like a dog and was covered in seaweed and horse mussels."

Note that sea monsters love mussels. Faxaskrímsli, the red comb, is common in Arnarfjörður, and though it will toss a boat of sailors into its snort of scalding steam, it lives almost exclusively on a diet of mussels. I don't suppose the mane on its horse-like head attains its bright screaming red because of the mussels, the way flamingos are gray in their youth but blush orange and pink as they eat enough algae and crustaceans. But then carrots and watermelon are composed to change the color of our own skins, if only we ate enough of them, and the faxaskrímsli eats enough mussels to weigh in at twenty tons.

Note that the shore laddie may shake the shells on its body, but don't confuse it with a shell monster. The shell monster, or skeljaskrímsli, is stocky with a sizable head and an even more massive mouth, "not unlike a hippopotamus in size, only bigger." Yet it is named not for its mouth but for the sound of the shells—a part not properly its own—that cling to its scales or skins or wiry hairs. And if you do hear a skeljaskrímsli, its distinctive clinking and rattling as it comes ashore, do not confuse it with the jingle of rings on a sea bull's horns.

I AM TOLD THERE ARE FIVE FOUNDERS OF THE MONSTER Society. There were seven, briefly, at the start, but almost immediately five, and formally four of them now, though I personally can account for only two. There is a documentary filmmaker, a youth community coordinator, a graphic designer, a book designer, and a captain of a fishing ship. Four of them are from Bíldudalur. Three of those grew up together. Only one of them lives there still, but the others go back often enough you could be forgiven, at a glance, for not knowing which is which.

If you are trying to track them down, to round them up, to sort them out like specimens, you must know that they are always traveling. One about to go to Denmark, one just back. One always in Bíldudalur, or else one always in Reykjavík. One who will try to make it, but something's always just come up. I first met Arnar in Bíldó, in a corridor, between a shell monster and a shore laddie. It was entirely by coincidence, but having found him, I was sure he would lead me to more.

I kept trying, as politely as I could, to invite myself to a meeting. I wrote and I called. I extended my stay in Reykjavík. I left and came back. If the Monster Society existed because a group was always getting together, as if it restored something to be collected, to be mutually in the company of those few souls who could confirm the way you remembered it—then surely one could visit that clutch. A year passed. I had begun to despair of ever seeing more than one of them at all, when all my trouble and all their goodwill finally yielded the second and only other founder I have yet to meet. I met Maggi at his new home in Kópavogur one autumn afternoon, as the moon hung low and full over the water. We looked at the monster drawings he'd made while sailing Arnarfjörður to get the landscape just right.

By the time I met Maggi, I had made my peace. If any set of individuals should prove so alive in the telling yet untraceably elusive in the flesh, surely it would be the sea monster set. When I left his house, Maggi sent me away with a mock-up of a shore laddie he'd been working on, streamlined and bronze-colored and attached to a base like a little trophy for diligence. I did not know how to write it down on the customs form.

I think of the founders collectively, like Harpies or Fates

or heads on a Hydra—not interchangeable, but all of a piece. And because three of them started a band two beans before the five of them named themselves the Monster Society, I find I take the liberty of thinking of the founders collectively by the band name chosen by the three: Farfuglar. It means "the migrating birds." I find they make the most sense as birds, as things made by nature not just to leave but also to return. Perhaps they would lose their way, wouldn't come back, if they weren't such creatures. Before they could make themselves a Monster Society, these men made themselves birds.

THE BIRDS THOUGHT A LOT ABOUT THE ICELANDIC NAME for such a place: *skrímslasetur*. But the English version, the Sea Monster Museum, shifts the meaning of both roots. *Skrímsli* is just a monster, any monster, not specifically a sea monster per se. It leaves open the possibility of lake monsters and river monsters, and don't get me started on the monsters of land and air.

More important, though, *setur* is not a museum. It's something harder to translate, something like a *center*, "Like when you come together to study some special thing, for an event," the birds say. Which for a moment makes me imagine sea monsters in Lubbock, Texas, a dry place below an ocean of air that also skirts the word *museum* but is home to the Buddy Holly Center and the American Wind Power Center and the National Ranching Heritage Center. When pressed, the society translates its institution as something like the "settlement for knowledge about monsters." It is no easy meaning like the birds or the beans. It was not designed for the ease with which it might slip into another tongue.

They do not claim in Icelandic to be a museum. And

Icelandic museum professionals are insistent on this point, reminding me kindly, gently, tenaciously, that there are necessary conditions a museum must meet—and this is no museum. Museums by their definition collect, conserve, research, and communicate. The International Council of Museums formally adds the fifth mandate: exhibit. A museum that has nothing to collect, then, is not a museum. They are very clear on that.

But the Sea Monster Museum has already collected four thousand testimonials, and it isn't done yet. Perhaps the stories can be so alike, it sometimes seems like a smaller number. As one of the birds tells me, the shore laddie, or fjörulalli, is described very similarly across regions in this country that were for a very long time unconnected. As one of the birds asks me: How can that be?

In an era when Iceland's national museum conference recently convened roughly under the theme "We have enough" and many Icelandic museums are entirely frank that they have more than they want to take care of, that going forward they'll scale back, surely the absence of a physical collection altogether is one kind of virtue. Surely the Sea Monster Museum was just fortunate to leapfrog over all that baggage weighing other museums down. I know the look of a museum director after years of no staff, no funding, devoted to a collection they did not start, do not know how to keep forever, but are bound to. It is a breathtaking devotion. Surely, it would be maddening if it weren't just the way it is. But when I ask if this isn't a harbinger, a step forward, a sign of museums to come, the conversation always hits a wall. Nobody wants to talk yet about the museum of things you can't see.

*

FOUNDED IN 1937 TO CAN FOOD, GREEN BEANS IN PARTICULAR, the building on the harbor side of the road next to the little yellow church had also been a slaughterhouse and a shrimp factory and, most recently, a fish factory. When they went looking for a museum location, the birds found it "empty and full with bad smells."

Before the fish factory closed it had been drying cod heads to meet demand in Nigeria. The roof was going down, a sag about to break but not yet cracked enough to air out the place. There were ghosts, too, of course; lots of people had seen them, but that wasn't a problem at all.

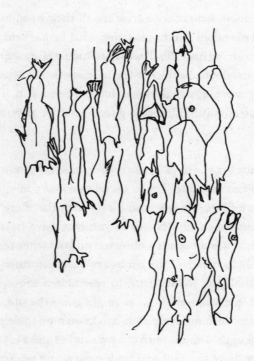

When the birds were boys in Bíldudalur, they heard some monster stories. "But maybe not so often." They were more likely to know about ghosts. Maybe your coworkers could supply the name in life of the apparition you met in the hallway. Maybe you caught a glimpse of one on the far side of a bridge. Maybe you took a boat trip as a teenager and the sea was completely even, everyone else asleep, when a heavy door swung open inexplicably.

As Arnar's father used to say, "Ghosts exist. I have seen it. Many times." But even Arnar's father couldn't understand his son and the rest of the birds building a museum for monsters. In the opinion of Arnar's dad: "Monsters are BS."

Of course fathers are a creature all their own, but I assume Arnar then said to his father what he has said to me: "This is our heritage. Shall we try to hide it? Be ashamed of it?" Or maybe he said what the tour says now: Music and dancing were quashed for six hundred years in Iceland, so as far as cultural heritage goes, "what we have are the stories."

THE SHORE LADDIE IS A KIND OF BUMBLER—OR ELSE IT runs as fast as a dog. Try to corral one and you will only chase it off into the sea. And it's not that the shore laddie seeks out pregnant women, as you may have heard, but rather that it is most often observed on land when the ewes are ready to breed. If the lambs are born deformed, more than usual, and if they tend to resemble a shore laddie, more than usual, well then you might guess the sire.

A lot of Icelandic monsters are known by their parentage. A skuggabaldur is born of a fox mother and a cat father. A nykur, they say, will foal underwater, and occasionally breeds with horses. The colts sired by these water horses with our typical mares will not have the nykur's backward fetlocks and hooves (recessive traits, it seems), but all will inherit its propensity to lie down when crossing water— which sounds harmless enough except for the way it pulls down riders into difficult crossings, drags them into currents fast and freezing, or if not the rider then all the packs and provisions, the nykur casting its burdens into the deep. No one suggests this as a test to root them out, but if you want one to bolt, know that it hates the sound of its own name.

Icelanders in general are keen on genealogy. One Icelander suggested to me, "We'd have to be. Not just because we are so few and you have to make sure you don't marry a relation, but if your great resource on this island is sheep, you better know how to husband." Which is to say, if sheep are feeding and clothing you on this arctic volcano of an outpost, you're going to become great record keepers to protect the line. If there aren't enough crops you can grow to feed yourselves, if your best bet is to turn the fields over to hay and hope it is enough to feed your livestock over winter, well then every unviable lamb and stillborn calf, so necessary, so deeply invested in, must, in the end, be answered for.

Back in 1932, "A cow in the Otradalur valley gave birth to a monster." It had two heads, their faces tapering to limp trunks. "General opinion was that the creature was the product of a union between its mother and a sea monster."

But the unknown need not be injurious. Sometimes the monster is something quite fine, though in those cases we tend to forget to call it a monster. The great breed of cows from Breiðavík, you might remember, descend from the one calf that Bjarni caught, once he gazed into the fog and saw a score of cattle and had the sense to catch the lagging calf while the rest of the herd, and a little boy herding them, disappeared beneath the sea. And Bjarni probably would have lost the calf later, the animal drawn back to its herd under the waves, had he not known immediately to hold it down and puncture the bladder between its nostrils so it could no longer live underwater. He altered this creature of two worlds so it would thereafter breathe only air.

THE BANK LOANED THE MONSTER SOCIETY THE MONEY TO buy the building, and the next summer the birds made the first working trip. There was a lot of work to do, and there were plenty who pitched in. I cannot imagine it except as a barn raising: the men putting up a new roof and laying down the new floors, the women bringing coffee and casseroles and baked goods in a massive potluck to keep them going, and the community pulled together on a scale we don't often get to witness in modern life. Think of them: all of them, the people who stayed and the people who left, all there and building something together, and everyone collapsing exhausted in the hot tub at the end of the day.

It was like this all that summer, as many as twenty-five guys going up to Bíldó for the weekend, traveling together, cooking together, weekend after weekend. It varied on any given weekend, of course, but the people in town who came to work were usually outnumbered by the people who came from far away. Maybe that's because so many people had left. Or maybe the people who had left needed this in a different way than the people who had stayed.

It's easy to imagine it wouldn't have mattered what they were making, that they all just needed a reason to be there, to come together, to make something with their own hands and feel bone tired when they stopped to rest. Whatever else it may produce, construction, necessarily, feels constructive. How can it not feel like progress when you have a hammer in your hands?

"WE THOUGHT THERE WOULD BE A SUBMARINE. IT WOULD move like this. And there would be screens, cod swimming by and like that. Maybe one or two monsters," the birds say. Then there would be a jolt. The submarine would shake and fail. The captain would shout. Maybe the passengers would scream. All would seem lost, but at the last moment, through cunning and bravery and sheer dumb luck, everyone would just barely escape.

The idea was to get the blood swimming. Visitors would be jostled and thrilled by one attraction or another, bounced along in wonder and delight and suspense until they landed in a final room that would give the stories some context to ground all that visceral sensation. They wrote the whole script. They mapped it all out.

In the plan, this final room is kind of a place to cool down after all that excitement, but it is also a final twist. The concept is elegant, indeed. It's have your cake and eat it, too. It was designed to give you what you craved: the fright and the spook. And just when you were getting full up on the shocking and the improbable, here was a room full of eyewitness accounts: films and texts and maps and audio recordings dismantling the tidy border between spectacle and history. Is it not most chilling of all, having been disarmed by entertainment and swathed in the safely impossible, to confront that there is reality behind the make-believe? You know what to do with your fear of a mask—but how do you begin to approach the bones that hold it up?

*

"WHEN THE HOUSE WAS ALMOST READY," THE BIRDS SAY, "then came this crash. It was dark times. Our plans were much bigger. But then this crash." The Icelandic economic miracle had been true in the sense that people did the things you do if you think there is the money to do them. They bought things. They took the loans the banks were so eager to make, and they started building. They say the optimism was intoxicating. They say that even if you were skeptical, even if you saw all the free money floating around and figured it was too good to last, you couldn't hear your own skepticism in the din of self-congratulatory hurrahs: a tiny long-struggling nation suddenly an international player! It was *such* a good story. Who could bear to hear the truth?

I sometimes wonder why there isn't a Museum of the 2009 Icelandic Banking Crisis and Economic Crash. It would show the jars of rhubarb jam people put up, having rediscovered, just growing there in ditches, this poison-leafed plant that can survive both abuse and neglect. It would feature the handmade sweaters that came into vogue, a thing that wasn't actually all that much cheaper to make, but that kept the hands busy, the mind occupied, the whole thing not just an object of comfort but also a kind of symbol of diligence and resourcefulness and self-sufficiency. There would be a display of how those same banks that brought everything down then repackaged themselves with new branding, each of them making a logo from a traditional Icelandic sweater design, as if they, too, were part of the resistance, as if banking should make you feel cozy. If individual volcanoes and earthquakes get their own museums here, what prevents us from having an institutional memory of all national disasters? Why don't we gather to call this thing by its name?

IT'S HARD TO SAY WHETHER THERE WOULD BE A SEA MONSTER Museum without the economic bubble. One could argue that the very availability of funding and the atmosphere of exceptional possibility helped tip it into being. But there is no doubt that the bubble bursting definitively shaped what the museum actually is.

"We had a loan. We had grants. We owed people for the work." The museum wasn't ready to open when the economy broke in 2009. There were no screens with cod swimming and the occasional monster floating by. There was no rocking submarine. There wasn't even the camera they planned to sink in the fjord, a thing you could control from the museum with a joystick to take a look around in real time. But it was clear things were going to get worse before they got better, and the birds thought, "If we don't open this summer, maybe we'll never open."

What they had, according to their plans, was that last room. A last with nothing to precede it. They had it because it had been the easiest thing to make. The stagecraft is exquisite, mind you; it's just that the physical demands of displaying oral history are flexible in a way that those of a submarine ride are not. And so the coda became the whole story. "What we thought would be just a little extra is the main thing."

There is now a café as you enter the museum. The café chairs fold distressed bronze-colored frames around crimson velvet seat cushions, a kind of shabby extravagance the place excels at. There are glass bottles of soda and beer, an apple cake, and a dark chocolate cake, all chilling in the slender refrigerated case. If you are lucky, the soup of the day is monster soup, but don't think that's just marketing—some days it's something else.

The tour begins in the café in front of a wide wooden door held closed by a weight on a string. The door is wonderfully squeaky, like the lid of a vampire's coffin, and opens from the café into a wide L-shaped hallway with a life-size mock-up of a monster waiting for you at the vertex. The atmosphere is not spooky, per se, but dim and weathered, with the urgency of a movie soundtrack in the hall. To get out of the corridor and into the main gallery, you open another door and suddenly stand face-to-face with a beast. I've heard shrieks.

The main gallery is a box of a room, a kind of steampunk library with two wicker chairs in front of a flat screen to watch clips from the documentary, an interactive map table with ornate fittings, a hanging globe, a taxidermied seal, a parlor-ready sofa patterned in a velvet floral, and in the corner an old radio the size of an end table, with glowing orange dial, rewired to tune in, click by click, to ten different monster stories.

The walls of the room are painted a blue wash with a red undercoat that shows through. The center of the room is a crescent-shaped bookcase, its cubbies on the outside of the curve filled with bones and bottles and leather-bound gilt-spine tomes. There are portraits and cubby-sized dioramas with accompanying text. The inner curve of the bookcase is much the same, but with the grid of cubbies scaled back, and a pair of screens fit in the cubbies showing more people telling their stories.

When the birds talk about this room as it was in 2009, they still sound anxious. They still seem to worry, all proof to the contrary, that it won't work. Arnar tells me, "We were very afraid to open just that, but we had to. Of course we always knew it would be the heart of it. But I never thought it would be enough."

MAYBE IT IS "THE HEIGHT OF A MAN OR A HAYSTACK." MAYBE it leaves tracks at high tide. Maybe you are sent to fetch something or are laying underwater telephone cables or you look up just as the vet arrives to tend to your sick cow.

Or you may meet it in a truce, you doing no harm to it and it doing no harm to you. In a six-oared boat you may run aground on a sea monster. Just you and your sister, out for a lark, may steer your skiff too close to it and turn back. But if you accidentally run over a monster while riding your horse home from church, the creature thrashing to defend itself, well, then both you and your horse will have a set of triple slash wounds to prove it. You will eventually recover. Your horse will be destroyed.

Kristján Oddsson was tending his flock when he saw a dark green creature with eyes the size of coffee cups. "When it moved, it waddled slowly, with its arms out in front." Árni Magnússon had set off on a foxhunt when he saw the beast, "claws on its feet like a frog." Þorbjörn Þórðarson was the local doctor who treated the badly burned sailors of the English trawler *Royal Dunn*, set upon as they were by a twenty-ton creature a good thirty feet long not including the tail or neck, a creature with "a roar like a bull" that "spewed poison from its nostrils on the crew."

But whether you shoot at it or batter it with a rock, whether you wound the creature or frighten it away, you will never take home a trophy. The skirmish will end, inevitably, with the monster fleeing, at last, into the safety of the sea.

Unless the problem is that you deign to leave its corpse unattended. The little sea horse of Arnarfjörður was found dead and washed ashore in 1827. It was a seal, essentially, a seal with flippers, except it had the rear legs and tail of a horse. The person who discovered it was aghast and confused and did not dare to touch it. By the next day it had disappeared. How much do we lose because we do not sense its impending impermanence, its essential ephemerality?

IF THERE IS NO MUSEUM; IF THERE IS NO STUFF; IF YOU NEED the things a museum can do but you've somehow neglected to amass a material history, somewhere overlooked the necessity of physical objects, just basically spaced on gathering the cache of touchstones to populate a memory palace of the thing you want no one to forget—what then?

The Sea Monster Museum never needed to be a museum of things—never could have been, never wanted to be. The evidence at hand is almost exclusively eyewitness accounts, and indeed this is not a museum that is trying to convince you that sea monsters even exist. They say it's just like the house next door, the yellow church: You can decide what you believe. It is a museum mindful of mystery, a museum of how what we count as known morphs over time. And this is hardly a dereliction of duty. It does enough work educating its visitors that these are stories we tell. What does it matter about the monsters? It is these stories that exist.

There are physical things in the museum, but they are not artifacts or specimens. Or rather, they are—the sperm

whale teeth and the cuttlefish cones—they're just not artifacts or specimens of monsters. There is an antique helmet,
a jug, a working balance with weights. There is a logbook
and a ship in a bottle and rolls of sealskin and a float of glass
buoys and a note in a bottle and a jawbone unhinged. The
doctor's kit, with all its capillary pipettes and cork stoppers
and rubber nipples and blood sugar standards, is an actual
vintage doctor's kit. It's there in the museum to reference
the doctor who treated the sailors scalded at sea by a red
comb, but it belonged to a different doctor, the grandfather
of one of the founders, a man with stories of his own.

If they were labeled differently, or in some cases labeled
at all, you might recognize this as a natural history museum, or a local history or maritime museum. But it is
something so rare you've perhaps never heard of one: an
oral history museum. Maybe you would have guessed that
such a thing doesn't exist.

IN THIS VALLEY THERE'S A STORY ABOUT GÍSLI, A MAN WHO
came to Bíldó only once, walked all the way from his farm
in Selárdalur with the express purpose of buying an organ,
the musical kind. Gísli wrote poetry, much of it about lone-
liness. They say he had a lonely cow. He had a famous hat,
found it on the shore, a hat with the top eaten away so he
knitted a new top for it and wore it the rest of his days.
He lived on the top floor of his house, long after the other
family members were gone and there were other rooms
to choose from, lived there with the organ and a drift of
papers.

Arnar and two friends once paid a visit, were invited
up for coffee, not that Gísli himself drank coffee in the

afternoon. Gísli pulled down a little aluminum pot, absolutely black, and proceeded to clean it with a pitch-black rag. Then he sat at the organ and played a hymn.

Once a foxhunter and his friend were passing by, and they stopped at Gísli's. The friend took a shine to a picture in Gísli's house. The friend was a collector, and Gísli was convinced to part with it. A few days later, they went back to return the picture. They couldn't bear thinking of him sitting there looking at the clean spot on the wall where the picture had always hung.

When Gísli died, there was a meeting to discuss turning his house into a museum. But when they approached the farmer who owned the house, they learned that the farmer had already emptied it. Swift as that—even the windows had been replaced. They knew, right in the beginning, that it should be a museum. And, almost as quickly, it was impossible.

"WHAT'S AT THE CENTER OF THE MUSEUM NOW WAS MEANT to be the serious, educational part," the birds say. "After you'd had an excitement, then you go to the serious part. But we are still on this stage: the serious part."

The Sea Monster Museum is a museum of expectations, of what is and what isn't, of what will and won't be. Some guests are disappointed. Some kids are still scared long after anything would have been prone to jump out or attack. Some visitors would surely have been happier if there had been that submarine. The museum proclaims itself as something specific enough, you think you know what it is. Indeed, without giving it any particular thought at all, you think you know what it must be. And this, it seems, is the problem.

It is museums that have taught me how much I love a thing that is exactly what it purports to be and also something else entirely. This works very much in the favor of the Museum of Icelandic Sorcery and Witchcraft and the Herring Era Museum and the Icelandic Phallological Museum. It should be similar for the Sea Monster Museum, the way it gives you both the tantalizing promise of the fantastic and the satisfaction of something solid and sober you didn't know would interest you. But somehow here the pivot is hard. Perhaps we are too invested in escaping what we know.

There is so much to savor in monster stories—their strangeness, their terror—but my favorite part, almost always, whether from the sagas or the present day, is the ritual establishment of the reliability of the source. *No one who knew Sigtryggur doubts the truthfulness of this account.* Or *Gísli maintained that Grímur was a truthful and honest man.* You don't even need someone else to vouch for you; you may report on yourself. *I saw this many years ago. I didn't tell it. But now I don't mind if people think I'm crazy.*

In Bíldó, the birds have new interviews to record. There are four more people willing to talk. They are people in their sixties, people older than that. The birds tell me about one very old man who, they stress, is still crystal clear. Another monster sighter, well, "He's not a good storyteller. That way, I know he'll never lie."

They were sober. The weather was good. The sun was out. We don't just tell stories about the monsters; we have to tell stories about how they were seen. It's as if the monsters don't exist on their own without us, are always tethered to being seen. These stories root so self-consciously in an assumption of skepticism, pretend to nothing if not a scrupulous report. You don't have to see the trolls building a chain of islands through the night, and you don't have to witness the gobbling up of naughty children by the Christmas Cat. But whether it be the farm girl or the foxhunter, someone has to see the sea monster.

There's a story about a camera set up on the shore. The point was to photograph a sea monster. There was a trip wire in the sand. The first photograph was a sheep. The second photograph was a farmer's leg. It was slow going. Someone had to reset the camera every shot. But there, in the third photograph, was an unidentified blur! The experimenters were satisfied it was a sea monster. They packed up their equipment without so much as taking photograph number four.

The museum has just such a camera on its shelves. Not everything was lost when an avalanche pummeled the photographer's garage and the photos and film stored there. But the point of the story, I think, is that we don't need to see the photograph. We just need the story of the people who did, who looked at the grains of silver and were convinced they knew enough.

"THIS IS THE FIRST IDEA," THE BIRDS SAY OF THE MUSEUM, OF this place built in joy out of grief. "There are still a lot of ideas, things that can come maybe later. Car rentals, bike rentals, boat trips." Which is to say, someone should set up some sea-monster-themed lodgings, now that the hostel in the harbor has closed, but the museum itself still needs attention.

It is a palpably physical place, and so there are things to fix. They need to add doors to the kitchen, for instance, expand the menu, do something to appease the foreigners always asking for fish. The foreigners don't ask for it, but you know what's delicious? Lamb's fat over fish, the birds tell me, with rye bread and butter. Maybe they'll try adding that.

They haven't forgotten about that remote-operated camera they wanted to scan the waters outside the museum. "Maybe we will do that," the birds still say about the camera. "When we can."

Back in Reykjavík is the very grand-sounding Icelandic Museum of Natural History. Don't get excited now that I've mentioned it; don't add it to your list—you can't go there. It's a collection and scholars study it, but without a place the public can actually access. You are not invited down to the rows of shelves, the dusty boxes. If the Sea Monster Museum doesn't really have things, the Icelandic Museum of Natural History doesn't really have a museum. It's all storage, no display. It is a big, old, probably venerable collection, and people have been talking about making it into a museum you could actually see for "so long it begins to sound like the wind."

Here at the Sea Monster Museum, the birds have no regrets. Not about the mortgage or the maintenance or how it all came off. But if they had known the shape of it, the sheer size—if they had known its longevity or the actual contours of this commitment—they would not have pursued it. They would have found it shocking and left it on the beach.

And as it is, they're still feeling out its possibility. They're still groping about for what all it might be. "We're trying to make this building something for the people," they tell me. This winter, the museum is open on Saturdays for guys to

watch football. One night a famous singer will perform.
There've been dance lessons and a pub trivia night. When
the church next door holds a particularly well-attended
funeral—when the town weeps for a sailor lost at sea or a
father who does not come home—the museum is there to
seat the overflow.

YOU MAY BE HUNTING A FOX OR GRAZING YOUR SHEEP OR
strolling along the shore when you meet the shore laddie.
You may see it in 1947 or 1915 or 1900 or around 1880. Guð-
mundur Hegalín saw one as a boy and called out to it, but
"the creature sauntered into the shallows and disappeared
back out to sea."

What did that little boy expect when he hailed the sea
monster? Was there something he wanted to ask? Did he
need to shout the way a dog needs to bark, or was this a
cue for communion, the way we cry to a countryman? Or
else was it the way I hear it, a plea for recognition, the way
we ache for a moment of grace but cannot contrive or convince grace that it should ache for us? And later, does the
man himself remember what, as a little boy, he desired?

WHEN THE BIRDS WERE BOYS, ONE OF THEM LIVED IN THE
middle of town and another one lived in the valley. Of
course there were ghosts everywhere. One night it was time
to part ways, go home for dinner, but how exactly to get
each one home?

When they came to the house of the boy who lived in
town, they walked right past it, together. They kept walking
until they had walked out of town. When they had walked
halfway between the town and the valley, between what
they knew and what they feared, they stopped and counted

to three. It is good to have a ritual. It is good to know these things. They counted to three and then each bolted, in a sprint. They ran in opposite directions. They ran screaming. They ran singing. They ran shouting at the top of their lungs. And they ran like this, crying out in the night, so each might hear the other, for as long as they possibly could.

The Museum of Seagull Tricks

I f there is a Museum of Seagull Tricks, it is run by one man
on a fishing boat puttering into the Húsavík harbor. It
keeps short hours. As our whale-watching boat drifts past
it, the fisherman leaning on the rail of his rig feels the weight
of us watching him, his boat, now that we are coming home
and too close to land to see any more whales and too far
around the rocky outcrop to glimpse another puffin.

He drops a handful of fish guts into the sea, and the gulls
that have been gathering in the air now dive and clatter in
waves of their own making. He takes two handfuls and
tosses them high against the sky, and another gust of birds
swoop and swallow and circle back, neither their feathers
nor the fish guts ever touching the water. Next the man extends his arm and holds up a chunk of fish flesh like a bea-
con, and a single flapping bird suspends itself in the air and
eats from his hand. We have begun to clap.

Exultant, defiant, the man holds up another chunk of fish,
perhaps higher this time, and the beat of all those wings
tightens to him. Such intent in these birds—such tense cunning and strike! It is all potential; anything could happen.
And then the man reaches out into the snugging swarm and
plucks a bird from the air. Seagulls may not be the most ex-
pressive of beasts, but this fowl in this moment is startled to
the brink of its bird brain, swivels its head and cranes its neck,
looking around wildly, not at the man so much as at the air

that has become hands and wool sweater fit just so around the bird, who has not until this moment thought of air or hands or wool sweaters, has thought only of fish and occasionally the sea but is now tucked under an arm and bewildered, perhaps consoled.

Our boat is much bigger than the fisherman's. From the railing of our deck, we look down at the scene and applaud. There are scores of us. We are zipped up in insulated blue onesies like astronauts or throw pillows, essentially snowsuits but waterproofed to protect us from the sea spray and edged in reflective tape so we can be seen if we topple overboard. We have been given hot chocolate and cinnamon rolls here in the calmer water, returning home, still swaddled in our suits, though we are not so cold without the wind on the open water and the speed of the boat.

Our faces—indeed our eyes, our hearts—are open. This display on the little boat has taken us completely by surprise, and we press to the railing and beam. The fisherman takes the seagull from under his arm and with two hands throws it into the sky. The gull flaps away furiously, all adrenaline and disdain, until finally, having shaken off the shock, it drifts back on the draft because, whatever it was that just happened, you never know—there might be more fish.

The fisherman looks back at us, returning our gaze. He slaps his hands together to say it's over, that's it, but we just continue to beam at him, enchanted. He waves us away. He draws a finger across his neck to say it's finished, no more, how many seagull tricks do you think there are, anyway? Yet we do not turn away. We do not go about our business and we don't shift our view to the port we have been sailing toward the whole time. We do not so much as toddle off to see if there's one last pastry left among the crumbs in the basket. The fisherman looks at us like we've missed the point.

In lieu of an encore, he turns his back to us and takes up anew the business of fish and nets and boats. He does not look at us again. Which I know because we remain at the railing, craning from that border's edge, adjusting our bodies and our gazes only so that we may keep the little fishing boat in view. And we continue to watch, snug in its thrall, long after there is anything left to see.

Acknowledgments

If you believe in beginnings, this whole endeavor was set in motion by the very existence of a Stanley Graduate Award for International Research—and because Lina Ferreira sent me a list. And because, before that, some other writer compiled that list. And because Garðar Johannesson, when given the opportunity, did not distract me with a single other fact.

I owe an obvious and immediate and indelible debt to the collectors, curators, directors, founders, staff, and their families who laid before me the marvels of Iceland's collecting and exhibition. Because of Sigurður's work, I thought there might be an essay. Because of Lilja's help, I knew there would be a book. Tinna Kvaran and Brooks Walker have made my eyes wide with wonder. Anita Elefsen and Örlygur Kristfinnsson astound me with their generosity. Stefanía and Álfdís Stefánsdóttir, Kristín Sigurgeirsdóttir, and Kristín Þuríður Sverrisdóttir opened doors for me. Sigríður Margrét Guðmundsdóttir and Kjartan Ragnarsson built a place I could walk through.

Every Icelander who has invited me to the kitchen table to hear their story has made it feel like a holy act; I am particularly humble before Þórkatla, Sveinn, Ingimar, Elsa Lísa, and the children beyond counting. The Monster Society— Arnar and Maggi especially—were worth the wait, not to mention Ingimar Oddson and Hallveig Ingimarsdóttir. Ingi

Hans was just taking the rhubarb jam off the stove when I knocked on the door. Josephine Wade and Einar Guðmundsson packed a picnic. Óddny Eir was waiting at the café on a stormy day. Þorvaldur Friðriksson found time to talk with me on a park bench. Valgeir Þorvaldsson came in from the haying and made me coffee under a peaked attic roof. Íris Ólöf Sigurjónsdóttir and Hjörleifur Hartarson introduced me to the delight of a book owned only by people who would never need to read it. Thank you, consummate hosts Bjarni Gunnarsson and Heida Simonardóttir, for making a backward museum. Thank you, Jón Allansson and Eiríkur Hilmar Eiríksson, for help with the buffalo coat. Thank you, Valdís Einarsdóttir, for the gravestone of a horse in the modern kitchen, and—as you say is the case whenever a very curious child asks very good questions—for giving me a dog.

The care and scholarship of Sigurjón Baldur Hafsteinsson and Magnús Rafnsson guided my own. Jökull Saevarsson reminds me that it's foreigners who make maps. Margrét Hallgrímsdóttir gave me the heaviest of all the museum books I have carried across Iceland, and has left me convinced that while I'm not particularly interested in one barber's chair, I would like to see all ten in the collection—one in every color.

Among the wealth of museum workers and storytellers who lent their vast expertise, let me mention Smári Ólason, Steinunn Sveinsdóttir, Þóra Björk Ólafsdóttir, Agusta Kristofersdóttir, Hildur Ploder Vigfusdóttir, Inga Lara Baldvinsdóttir, Sigrún Kristjánsdóttir, Lilja Arnadóttir, Ófeigur "Kyle's got an Icelander!" Sigardsson, and Sigrún Guðmundsdóttir of the Reykjavík textile collection, with its bowls of ribbons and buttons in jars and the apron sewed as a pocket to keep one's knitting in.

Guðrun, the brilliant cultural matchmaker of Iceland, and Rúnar have become touchstones to so many people I needed to meet and things I needed to know. Katrín and Svava have created the warmest destination on the island, where I felt at home even before they gifted me a mantra: There will always be waffles. Quentin and Sylvia and Sessý gave me shelter to edit. Solveig said to take the next bus. Óskar can be heard all the way upstairs admonishing his cousins: "Ekki hafa hátt! Við erum með gesti!" Andrea and Melanie (who let me drive), Gary (who forbid it), and Matt (who rides a coattail most elegantly) each helped me better see a place I already loved.

Erica Mena believed unfailingly, enthusiastically, and wholeheartedly in this project from its first words. Anomalous Press dressed it in chapbooks. Lee Marchalonis and Annie Nilsson honored it with images. Gretchen Greene designed custom endpapers. Elena Passarello, Matthew Gavin Frank, Jón Gnarr, Kurt Caswell, Barry Lopez, David Searcy, and Ben Fountain bore witness. Fowzia Karimi single-handedly established my devotion to squiggly birds—and then put a pen in my hands.

The writing has found its way because of Lina, again, though she denies me the strings of the murder board; Jenny, who does not doubt that digression is the point; Amanda and Sarah, who coined the shorthand Kendra-on-a-bike; Lisa, who finds herself in a skiff; Kristen and Ariel, who are effortlessly savvy; Anna, who says wait; Garnette, who says call even later; Stephanie, who can spot a unicorn; and Inara and Kisha and Angela, who anchor the victories.

Kim, you dark angel, how many of these essays first debuted at your dinner table? Karan, thank you for adding your living room to the cause. John Freeman, how right you were to introduce me to Duvall Osteen. Duvall, I can't imagine any of this without you, without the way you see this book for everything it is.

John Siciliano and Anne Meadows, what an honor it is to have the lavish attention of you both. John, what a gift it has been to be told to draw.

Barbara, Margy, Tom, and Dan, there's no forgetting your faith in collections yet unknown. Jim and Peggy, thank you for space on the porch swing. Early versions of these essays have been read at the Wild Detectives, Nordic House, Gamut Gallery, and the Sowell Family Collection at Texas Tech—and by the invitation of Inner Moonlight, Pegasus Reading Series, Spiderweb Salon, and NonfictioNow. This book is in memory of Sigurður Atlason and Ljósbjörg Petra María Sveinsdóttir, who were lost during its writing; and Sigurgeir Stefansson, Samúel Jónsson, and the Rev. Jón M. Guðjónsson, who went before.

Like any collection, this one exists and has flourished with the love of my family. This book is for Alice, who has noticed books have dedications, and would like one about unicorns in the library dedicated to her.

Appendix Ð

MUSEUMS VISITED—EVEN IF ONLY
BRIEFLY—IN THIS BOOK

BYGGÐASAFNIÐ HVOLL/HVOLL FOLK MUSEUM
Karlsrauðatorg, 620 Dalvík

BYGGÐASAFNIÐ Í GÖRÐUM/AKRANES FOLK MUSEUM
Garðaholt 3, 300 Akranes

DRAUGASETRIÐ/ICELANDIC WONDERS—GHOSTS, ELVES,
TROLLS, AND NORTHERN LIGHTS
Hafnagötu 9, 825 Stokkseyri

ELDFJALLASAFNIÐ STYKKISHÓLMI/VOLCANO MUSEUM
Aðalgata 6, 340 Stykkishólmur

FRAKKAR Á ÍSLANDSMIÐUM/THE FRENCH MUSEUM
Hafnargata 12, 750 Fáskrúðsfjörður

FUGLASAFN SIGURGEIRS/SIGURGEIR'S BIRD MUSEUM
Ytri-Neslöndum, 660 Mývatn

GALDRASÝNING Á STRÖNDUM/MUSEUM OF ICELANDIC
SORCERY AND WITCHCRAFT
Höfðagata 8–10, 510 Hólmavík

HIÐ ÍSLENZKA REÐASAFN/ICELANDIC PHALLOLOGICAL MUSEUM

Héðinsbraut 3a, Húsavík (at time of writing)
Laugavegur 116, 105 Reykjavík (at time of publication)

HVALASAFNIÐ Á HÚSAVÍK/HÚSAVÍK WHALE MUSEUM

Hafnarstétt 1, 640 Húsavík

HVALASÝNINGIN/WHALES OF ICELAND

Fiskislóð 23–25, 101 Reykjavík

LANDNÁMSSETUR ÍSLANDS/SETTLEMENT CENTER

Brákarbraut 13–15, 310 Borgarnes

LANDSBÓKASAFN ÍSLANDS–HÁSKÓLABÓKASAFN/NATIONAL LIBRARY OF ICELAND

Arngrímsgata, 107 Reykjavík

LITLA HVALASAFNIÐ/THE SMALL WHALE MUSEUM

Ferstikluland, 301 Hvalfjarðarsveit

LÍSTASAFN SAMÚELS JÓNSSONAR SELÁRDAL/SAMÚEL JÓNSSON ART MUSEUM

Brautarholt, 465 Bíldudalur

MENNINGARMIÐSTÖÐ ÞINGEYINGA/DISTRICT CULTURAL CENTRE

Stórigarður 17, 640 Húsavík

NÁTTÚRUMINJASAFN ÍSLANDS/ICELANDIC MUSEUM OF NATURAL HISTORY

Brynjólfsgata 5, 107 Reykjavík

PÁLSHÚS SAFNAHÚS/PÁLSHÚS MUSEUM
Strandgata 4, 625 Ólafsfjörður

SAFNAHÚS BORGARFJARÐAR/BORGARFJÖRÐUR MUSEUM
Bjarnarbraut 4-6, 310 Borgarnesi

SAGNHEIMAR BYGGÐASAFN/SAGNHEIMAR FOLK
MUSEUM
Safnahúsinu við Ráðhúströð, 900 Vestmannaeyjar

SÍLDARMINJASAFN ÍSLANDS/HERRING ERA MUSEUM
Snorragata 10, 580 Siglufjörður

SJÓMINJA- OG SMIÐJUSAFN JÓSAFATS HINRIKSSONAR/
JÓSAFAT HINRIKSSON MARITIME MUSEUM
Egilsbraut 2, 740 Neskaupstað

SKÓGASAFN/SKÓGAR MUSEUM
Safnavegur 1, 861 Skógar

SKRÍMSLASETRIÐ/ICELANDIC SEA MONSTER MUSEUM
Strandgötu 7, 465 Bíldudalur

SMÁMUNUSAFN SVERRIS HERMANSSONAR/SVERRIR
HERMANNSSON'S SUNDRY COLLECTION
Sólgarður, 601 Akureyri

SPÁKONUHOF/MUSEUM OF PROPHECIES
Oddagata 6, 545 Skagaströnd

STEINASAFN PETRU/PETRA'S STONE COLLECTION
Fjarðarbraut 21, 755 Stöðvarfjörður

SÖGUSAFNIÐ/SAGA MUSEUM
Grandagarður 2, 101 Reykjavík

SÖGUSETRIÐ/SAGA CENTRE
Hlíðarvegur 14, 860 Hvolsvöllur

VESTURFARASETRIÐ Á HOFSÓSI/ICELANDIC EMIGRATION
CENTER
Kvosin, 566 Hofsós

ÞEKKINGARSETUR SUÐURNESJA/SUDURNES SCIENCE AND
LEARNING CENTER
Garðskagavegur 1, 245 Suðurnesjabær

ÞJÓÐMINJASAFN ÍSLANDS/NATIONAL MUSEUM OF ICELAND
Suðurgata 41, 101 Reykjavík

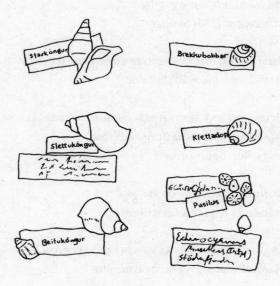

Appendix Þ

COLLECTION OF DRAWINGS

p. 111 *Ardea cinerea* (gráhegri/grey heron legs, that the sailor may return), collection of Skógasafn, Skógar

p. 133 Comb, scissors, pin, collection of Skógasafn, Skógar

p. 143 *Silene uniflora* (holurt/sea campion), Höfn

p. 145 Nets and floats, collection of Fuglasafn Sigurgeirs, Mývatn

p. 150 Herring girl aprons, Siglufjörður

p. 159 Reflection of the hotel in the harbor, Siglufjörður

p. 172 Dresses in the dormitory, collection of Síldarminjasafn Íslands, Siglufjörður

p. 176 *Empetrum nigrum* (krækiber/crowberry), Skagaströnd

p. 177 *Histocidaris purpurata* (ígulker/urchin), collection of Sagnheimar Byggðasafn, Heimaey

p. 184 *Papaver radicatum* (melasól/Arctic poppy), Hólmavík

p. 190 Coffee cups, Galdrasýning á Ströndum, Hólmavík

p. 199 *Aphrodita aculeata* (sea mouse), collection of Galdrasýning á Ströndum, Hólmavík

p. 204 Lístasafn Samúels Jónssonar Selárdal

p. 207 *Buccinum undatum* (beitukongur/whelk), Ísafjardarbær

p. 212 *Ascophyllum nodosum* (klóþang/rockweed), Arnarfjörður

p. 221 *Gadus morhua* (þorskur/cod heads hanging to dry outside Sagnheimar Byggðasafn), Heimaey

p. 235 *Arctica islandica* (kúfskel/Icelandic cyprine), collection of Skrímslasetrið, Arnarfjörður

p. 241 *Fucus vesiculosus* (bóluþang/bladder wrack), Arnarfjörður

p. 246 *Ardea cinerea* (grárhegri/grey heron in private stone collection), Djúpivogur

p. 250 *Sipho glaber, Buccinum hydrophanum, Buccinum undatum, Cepaea hortensis, Littorina saxatilis, Echinocyamus pusillus, Capulus hungaicus, Pyrena rosacea, Cylichna insculpta* (starkóngur/slender spindle shell, slettukóngur/whelk, beitukóngur/common whelk, brekkubobbi/white-lipped snail, klettadoppa/rough periwinkle, and pusilus/pea urchin, hnífilbobbi/bonnet shell, mardúfa, krostúfa/bubble snails), collection of Steinasafn Petru, Stöðvarfjörður

A. Kendra Greene is a writer and artist who has worked at the Museum of Contemporary Photography, the Chicago History Museum, the University of Iowa Museum of Natural History, and the Dallas Museum of Art, where she was a writer in residence. She has an MFA in nonfiction and a graduate certificate in book arts from the University of Iowa and has received a Fulbright grant, a Jacob K. Javits Fellowship, and a Harvard Library Innovation Lab Fellowship. She lives in Dallas, where she is a visiting assistant professor at the University of Texas, a guest artist at Nasher Sculpture Center, and an associate editor at *Southwest Review*.